ATTITUDES TOWARD DEATH AND FUNERALS

Amy Seidel Marks

Bobby J. Calder

CMS The Center for Marketing Sciences

J. L. KELLOGG GRADUATE SCHOOL OF MANAGEMENT

NORTHWESTERN UNIVERSITY

ATTITUDES TOWARD DEATH AND FUNERALS
was conducted through a grant from the

National Research and Information Center
1614 Central Street
Evanston, Illinois 60201
Dr. Joe A. Adams, Director

CONTENTS

Executive Summary

This study examines how consumers think and feel about death and funerals, and updates a comparable study done in 1974 by the Casket Manufacturers of America. The information was gathered from five focus group interviews — four held in Chicago and one held in Los Angeles — and from an extensive mail survey that was completed by 1121 people. A summary of the overall findings is presented below, and the location of a fuller discussion of each finding is shown.

EXPERIENCE WITH FUNERALS, WAKES AND VISITATION/CALLING HOURS

3

ATTITUDES TOWARD FUNERAL SERVICES

6

ATTITUDES TOWARD CASKETS

7

8

9

I. Introduction

1. Objective

This research seeks to increase understanding of how consumers think and feel about death and funerals. It explores people's attitudes toward attending funerals, preplanning, funeral services, funeral homes, caskets, disposition of the body, and pricing. The objective is to obtain an in-depth understanding of the nature and causes of these consumer attitudes.

The research updates and extends an earlier 1974 study for the Casket Manufacturers Association of America (CMA) by Roger D. Blackwell and W. Wayne Talarzyk. The 1974 CMA study may be thought of as providing a benchmark from which to assess changes in consumer attitude. New questions were added in the current research, and some questions were reworded to provide better measures of consumer attitude, but wherever possible an effort was made to achieve some degree of comparability with the 1974 results.

2. Methodology

A two stage research design was employed. The first stage was qualitative in nature. Five focus group interviews were conducted — four in Chicago and one in Los Angeles. The groups consisted of eight to ten people selected at random from different communities.

The interviews followed an unstructured, open discussion format. The moderator controlled the discussion only to the extent of making sure that topics of interest were covered. The group process results in a high level of spontaneity and candor. The interaction among the participants reveals their attitudes in a natural way unbiased by a specific question and answer format.

Each focus group session lasted over two hours. Participants were paid a nominal amount ($20) for their time. The sessions were tape recorded for analysis as well as video taped.

The second phase of the study consisted of a mail survey. Questionnaires were mailed to 1600 respondents. Because females are more likely to return mail questionnaires, 950 were sent to males and 650 to females. Of the total 1600 questionnaires, 1121 were returned. The return rate was 34% (381) for males and 66% (740) for females. Although the survey was long, less than 50 people out of the 1121 refused to answer (0.4%) any given question. A copy of the questionnaire giving the exact wording of each question is appended to this report.

All interviewing was completed in the winter of 1981.

3. Scope of the findings

For this report to be read in proper perspective, the reader should be acquainted with the fact that the focus group interview is a research technique designed to provide in-depth rather than statistical analysis. The goal is to discover patterns in the experiences of people that explain their reactions as consumers. These patterns concern how consumers see and explain things in their own terms and from their own frame of reference.

Quotes from the focus group interview are included in this report to convey the way in which respondents expressed themselves. The reader can, accordingly, better judge the exact tenor of people's responses. All quotes are typical in that they are similar to those made by a number of people.

The strength of the focus group interview is in the depth of insight it provides. The technique is obviously limited as to the number of people who can be interviewed and geographical coverage. The mail survey, however, provides a way of extending the focus group results to a larger sample. The questionnaire used in this research was a direct outcome of the focus groups.

Mail surveys are well suited to obtaining the kind of extensive information sought in this research. Respondents can be presented with a large number of questions with detailed answer formats. Such surveys do not yield samples as statistically reliable as telephone surveys, but telephone surveys are of necessity limited in scope and depth. The use of a mail survey in this research is consistent with the objective of obtaining a deeper understanding of consumer attitudes.

Mail surveys are primarily biased against representing males and lower income groups. The bias against males was compensated for in this research by employing statistical weighting. The responses from males were multiplied by 1.942 so that they counted the same as the more numerous female responses. This weighting in effect produced a sample of 1480 respondents, consisting of 740 males and 740 females.

The number of lower income respondents in the survey was too low to employ weighting as a correction. For this reason, respondents with family incomes of under $8,000 were omitted from the analyses. This report is properly interpreted as a study of the population with above $8,000 income.

The study also appears to slightly under-represent Southerners. But, as shown by the table below, the study seems on the whole to reflect the geographical breakdown of the population.

	Region	Census %	Mail Survey %
East	N England	5.5	6.1
	M Atlantic	16.8	17.2
	Total East	**22.3**	**23.3**
Midwest	EN Central	19.0	19.5
	WN Central	8.0	9.8
	Total Midwest	**27.0**	**29.3**
South	S Atlantic	16.1	14.3
	ES Central	6.5	4.9
	WS Central	10.1	9.1
	Total South	**32.7**	**28.3**
West	Mountain	4.7	4.5
	Pacific	13.3	14.5
	Total West	**18.0**	**19.0**

In general, the results of the mail survey are less important for providing precise estimates of population frequencies than for revealing patterns in people's thinking.

II. Experience With Funerals, Wakes and Visitation/ Calling Hours

1. Attendance at funerals is high, but declining

Funeral attendance is, on the whole, high. Only 12.2% of the people surveyed had not attended a funeral in the past five years. Almost a third had attended five or more funerals. However, this is a decrease from the number of funerals that people in the 1974 CMA study reported attending.

NUMBER OF FUNERALS ATTENDED IN THE PAST FIVE YEARS

	% 1981		% 1974	
None	12.2		7.1	
1-4	55.8		53.2	
5-9	19.5 ⎤		24.2 ⎤	
10-14	5.7 ⎟ 32.0		8.1 ⎟ 39.7	
15-19	2.1 ⎟		2.0 ⎟	
20 or more	4.7 ⎦		5.4 ⎦	

Those who live in the West (either the Pacific or Mountain region) are less likely to have attended a funeral than those living in other parts of the U.S.

PERCENT IN EACH ZONE WHO HAVE NOT ATTENDED A FUNERAL IN THE PAST FIVE YEARS

	%
West	21.3
South	11.4
Midwest	8.2
East	10.7

Moreover, there has been an increase, since the 1974 CMA study, in people in each geographic region who have not attended a funeral in the last five years.

PERCENT IN EACH REGION WHO HAVE NOT ATTENDED A FUNERAL IN THE PAST FIVE YEARS

		% 1981	% 1974*	% Increase
West	Pacific	21.1	15.0	6.1
	Mountain	22.0	11.0	11.0
South	WS Central	11.8	8.0	3.8
	ES Central	8.2	5.0	3.2
	S Atlantic	12.2	6.0	6.2
Midwest	WN Central	6.1	6.0	0.1
	EN Central	9.3	5.0	4.3
East	M Atlantic	11.1	4.0	7.1
	N England	9.8	7.0	2.8

In terms of all people surveyed, those who were 45 years of age or older had attended more funerals than younger people.

Number of Funerals Attended	% Under 45 Years**	% 45 Years and Over**
None	15.3	10.0
1-4	66.8	47.7
5 or more	18.0	42.2

* These results are unweighted and represent females disproportionately.
** These columns and others throughout the report do not sum to 100.0% because of error incurred in rounding the individual percentages in the column.

20

Those who rated themselves as rather religious (either "very religious" or "religious") also had attended more funerals than those who were less religious.

Number of Funerals Attended	% Not Very Religious	% Rather Religious
None	14.6	10.7
1-4	65.1	49.2
5 or more	20.2	40.2

Although there was not much difference among people with particular religious affiliations in numbers of funerals attended, those who indicated they had no religious beliefs or were agnostic or atheist were almost three times as likely as others to have attended no funerals in the past five years. Of those with no religious beliefs or who were agnostic or atheist, 38.8% had attended no funerals, which is double the finding of 19% in the 1974 CMA study. Supplemental Table 1 provides further demographic breakdowns.

2. Attendance at wakes or visitation/calling hours is higher than attendance at funerals.

Attendance at wakes or visitation/calling hours is also very high. There was a tendency to attend more wakes or visitation hours than funerals, with 42.5% of those surveyed having been to five or more wakes/visitations as compared to only 32% having been to five or more funerals.

NUMBER OF WAKES/VISITATIONS/CALLING HOURS ATTENDED IN THE PAST FIVE YEARS

	%		%
None	19.0	10-14	10.4
1-4	38.5	15-19	4.1
5-9	20.2	More than 20	7.8

Total — More than 5: 42.5%

People in the West, however, differ greatly from all others in their experience with wakes or visitation periods. Almost one-half of the people from the West had not attended a wake/visitation, and only a total of 18.4% had attended five or more.

NUMBER OF WAKES/VISITATIONS/CALLING HOURS ATTENDED BY THOSE FROM THE WEST IN THE PAST FIVE YEARS

	%		%
None	47.5	10-14	3.1
1-4	34.1	15-19	0.5
5-9	13.0	20 or more	1.8

Total — More than 5: 18.4%

The focus group interview held in California indicated that many people there had attended an "open house" at the home of the deceased or a neighbor after the funeral service, rather than a wake or visitation period before the funeral.

"Usually the neighbors think enough of you that they have a buffet and all that kind of stuff."

"This gentleman friend of ours that just passed away in November, his widow asked us to come over (after the funeral). They do that all the time, I think, at that particular time. They like some friends around."

Lack of attendance at wakes/visitations in the West may in part be due to such informal arrangements.

22

Those who were under 45 years of age had attended fewer wakes or visitation hours in the past five years than those who were 45 years or older. Over one-fourth of the younger group had not attended a wake/visitation period whereas only 12.4% of the older group had not attended any. Only 27.9% of the younger group had gone to five or more wakes/visitation hours whereas 53.7% of the older group had gone to five or more.

NUMBER OF WAKES/VISITATION/ CALLING HOURS ATTENDED

	% Under 45 Years	% 45 Years or Older
None	27.4	12.4
1-4	44.7	33.8
5 or more	27.9	53.7

Those with a high school education or less and those who were less religious also were somewhat more prone to have gone to no wakes/ visitation hours or to have attended fewer wakes/visitation hours than were those with more education and those who were not religious. Supplemental Table 2 provides further demographic breakdowns.

3. Most of the funerals people attend are for non-immediate relatives, close personal friends, and acquaintances.

Respondents were asked how many funerals they had attended for specific categories of people. A majority had attended funerals for non-immediate relatives, for close personal friends, and for acquaintances or other people. Attendance at funerals for more immediate family members was less common. Only 2.7% had attended the funeral of a spouse.

23

CATEGORIES OF FUNERAL ATTENDANCE*

	%		%
Other Relative	59.5	Brother/Sister	11.3
Close Personal Friend	51.6	Mother	11.1
Acquaintance/Other	50.9	Spouse	2.7
Grandparent	16.5	Son/Daughter	2.1
Father	12.5		

NOTE: Percentages do not sum to 100% because of multiple responses.

As might be expected, most of those who had attended a spouse's funeral were women and were 45 years of age or older. Most of those who had attended funerals for parents or siblings were 45 years of age or older, whereas most of those who had attended funerals for grandparents in the past five years were under 45 years of age.

The most notable difference among those attending the first three categories of funerals were in terms of region and age. Around two-thirds of those from the East and Midwest had gone to funerals for non-immediate relatives, whereas only about half of those from the South and West had done so.

ATTENDANCE OF FUNERALS
FOR NON-IMMEDIATE RELATIVES

	% East	% Midwest	% South	% West
None	30.0	37.4	45.0	52.3
One or More	70.0	62.6	55.0	47.7

Almost two-thirds of those 45 years or older had attended a funeral for a close personal friend, whereas only one-third of those under 45 had done so. (See Supplemental Tables 3 to 11 for additional cross tabulations.

Respondents were also questioned about the funeral that they had attended most recently in the past five years. Slightly less than a quarter of the most recent funerals attended were for immediate family members.

PERSON FOR WHOM THE FUNERAL MOST RECENTLY ATTENDED

	%		%
Other Relative	28.0	Father	3.1
Close Personal Friend	23.0	Spouse	1.7
Acquaintance/Other	25.0	Son/Daughter	1.0
Grandparent	9.0		
Brother/Sister	4.5	**Cumulative Total,**	
Mother	4.4	**Last 6 Categories**	**23.7**

The demographic differences noted for descriptions of attendance at each kind of funeral basically held true for attendance of the most recent funeral. For instance, most of the respondents whose most-recently-attended funeral was for grandparents were under 45 years of age. (See Supplemental Table 12 for other breakdowns of demographic characteristics.)

4. Recently attended funerals were perceived as traditional and well done.

The vast majority of the funerals recently attended by respondents were traditional in nature. For example, the body of the deceased was usually buried in the ground.

HOW THE BODY WAS PUT TO REST

	%		%
Burial in the ground	90.8	Entombment above ground	1.7
Cremation, other than burial	2.6	Donation to science	0.3
Cremation, burial in the ground	1.8	Burial at sea	0.2
		Other	0.4
		Don't recall	2.1

25

Most of the funerals involved a wake or visitation/calling hours, and most of those surveyed attended this.

ATTENDANCE AT THE FUNERAL HOME BEFORE THE FUNERAL SERVICE DURING THE VISITATION/ CALLING HOURS OR WAKE

	%
Yes	71.8
No, although there was visitation/calling hours/wake	18.9
Total first two categories	**90.7**
No, there was no visitation/calling hours/wake	8.0
Don't recall	1.2

A majority of the funeral services were held at a funeral home, although more than a third were held in a church or synagogue.

WHERE THE FUNERAL SERVICE WAS HELD

	%		%
Funeral home	52.4	Other	0.3
Church or synagogue	39.2	Don't recall	1.0
Cemetery	7.1		

Most of the funerals were estimated to have had 40 or more people in attendance.

NUMBER OF PEOPLE ATTENDING

	%		%
Less than 10	1.1	80 or more	34.6
Between 10 and 39	23.5	Don't recall	4.5
Between 40 and 79	36.5		

26

In a majority of the funerals, limousines were used to transport the family and/or close friends of the deceased.

USE OF LIMOUSINES

	%		%
Two or more	30.2	None	32.5
One	29.0	Don't recall	8.3

Four or more flower arrangements were present at most of these funerals, with two-thirds of all funerals having more than a dozen present.

PRESENCE OF FLOWER ARRANGEMENTS

	%		%
More than a dozen	66.4	None	2.4
Several (4-11)	22.3	Don't recall	2.1
Only 1, 2 or 3	6.7		

The casket was present in almost all cases during at least some part of the funeral service or visitation/calling hours, and was open in most cases.

DURING SOME PART OF THE FUNERAL SERVICE OR VISITATION OR CALLING HOURS, THE CASKET WAS:

	% Yes	% No	% Don't Recall
Present	96.1	3.5	0.4
Open	84.3	14.4	1.3

Over one-third recalled the casket at the most recent funeral attended as being metal, with precious metal and wood designated as next most common. However, a third did not recall what material the casket was made out of.

PERCEPTION OF CASKET MATERIAL

	%		%
Metal	37.7	Fiberglass	0.9
Precious metal	18.0	Other	1.0
Wood	11.6	Don't recall	30.7

Results from a similar question in 1974 are shown below.

PERCEPTION OF CASKET MATERIAL IN 1974

	%
Metal	37.4
Polished hardwood	15.7
Wood, covered with cloth	5.1
Plain wood	1.6
Total wood	**22.4**
Fiberglass or other material	3.7
Do not recall	34.6
No casket present	0.3
I have not attended a funeral	1.6

In the earlier study, almost twice as many, 22.4%, reported the casket as being made of wood, although that category was actually broken into three different kinds of wood. Although 37.4% reported metal to have been used in 1974, this is not necessarily comparable to the percentage mentioned above for metal because precious metal may well have been included in this answer, since it was not an option in the 1974 study. (Inclusion of "no casket present" and "non-attendance" options in the 1974 study might also slightly distort the comparability of the 1974 findings with the current ones, although less than 2.0% selected this option.) The number who could not remember the casket material in 1981 was comparable to the number who could not recall it in the 1974 study. In general, comparison of the 1974 results with the current findings shows a shift away from wood toward metal.

Most of the funeral services recently attended by the respondents did involve a service at the cemetery and two-thirds of the respondents attended it.

ATTENDANCE OF A SERVICE
AT THE CEMETERY

	%
Attended	65.6
Did not attend	20.9
No service	12.1
Don't recall	1.4

Most people thought the funeral was at least reasonably well done, and over half of the total surveyed thought it was very well done.

REACTION TO THE FUNERAL
MOST RECENTLY ATTENDED

	%
Very well done	57.6
Reasonably well done	20.5
Total first two categories	**78.1**
Didn't stand out one way or another	16.9
Somewhat poorly done	1.1
Very poorly done	0.4
Don't recall or no opinion	3.5

5. About a quarter of those surveyed had arranged a funeral, and most of the funerals had been for parents or other close family members.

Around a quarter (25.9%) of all respondents had personally arranged a funeral at a funeral home. Respondents were asked how many funerals they had arranged for specific categories of people. About half of the total funerals arranged had been for parents and another quarter had been for close family members. Only 7.6% of the respondents had made arrangements for a spouse.

FUNERAL ARRANGEMENTS MADE DURING THE PAST FIVE YEARS (FOR RESPONDENTS PERSONALLY ARRANGING A FUNERAL)

	Number	% of the Total Funerals Arranged
Mother	126	25.8
Father	119	24.3
Other relative	81	16.6
Brother/sister	40	8.2
Spouse	37	7.6
Grandparent	27	5.5
Close personal friend	26	5.3
Son/daughter	25	5.1
Acquaintance/other	8	1.6
Total funerals arranged	**489**	**100.0**

As might be expected, women and those over 45 were most likely to have arranged a spouse's funeral. Most of those arranging funerals for parents, siblings or children were 45 years of age or older, whereas most of those making arrangements for grandparents were under 45 years of age. (See Supplemental Tables 13-22 for further crosstabulations.*)

6. People making funeral arrangements tend to share the decision-making with others; a majority are accompanied to the funeral home by two to four other people.

When asked specifically about the most recent funeral they had arranged, less than a third of those who had made recent arrangements were the primary decision maker. Most had either participated equally with others or had only a partial role in the decision making, with others having a more important role.

ROLE IN MAKING FUNERAL ARRANGEMENTS (FOR RESPONDENTS PERSONALLY ARRANGING A FUNERAL)

	%
Primary decision maker	29.5
Participated equally with others	44.4
Participated, but others had a more important role	20.9
Participated by carrying out preexisting detailed plans	5.2

Exceptions to this pattern occurred for those arranging a spouse's funeral, where the majority, 69.1%, were the primary decision makers. Also, for those arranging a close friend's funeral, 55.8% were the primary decision makers. And those arranging another relative's funeral varied from the norm in that 47.5% reported that others had had a more important role in the decision making.

* *Respondents were also asked to indicate what kind of funeral they had arranged most recently. The results so closely resembled the results for total funerals arranged reported above, they are not repeated here but are documented in Table 22.*

The majority of respondents who had made recent funeral arrangements were accompanied to the funeral home by two to four other people. Only 8.3% went by themselves. Of those arranging a spouse's funeral, however, 20.5% went alone.

NUMBER OF PEOPLE ACCOMPANYING RESPONDENT TO THE FUNERAL HOME (FOR RESPONDENTS PERSONALLY ARRANGING A FUNERAL)

	%
None	8.3
One	23.8
2-4	52.4
5-7	12.7
More than 8	1.7
Don't recall	1.7

Of those who accompanied the respondent to the funeral home, and who had a role in the decisionmaking, most were close relatives of the deceased.

CO-DECISION MAKER ACCOMPANYING RESPONDENT TO THE FUNERAL HOME (FOR RESPONDENTS PERSONALLY ARRANGING A FUNERAL)

	%
Close relative of the deceased	89.6
Other relatives or friends	9.6
Clergyman	2.4
Attorney	0.6
Other	3.0
Don't recall	0.6

7. Over a fourth of those making funeral arrangements perceive the funeral director, as well as the immediate family, as having a role in the decision making.

When asked who else besides the people accompanying them to the funeral home had a role in deciding about arrangements, two categories of people were mentioned most: the person's own immediate family and the funeral director.

OTHER PEOPLE HAVING A ROLE IN DECIDING ABOUT ARRANGEMENTS (FOR RESPONDENTS PERSONALLY ARRANGING A FUNERAL)

	%		%
Immediate family	30.0	Attorney	1.4
Funeral director	29.5	Memorial society	—
Clergyman	10.2	Others	0.9
Other relative(s)	9.7	None	38.5
Friends	1.4	Don't recall	3.4

8. Usually the general wishes of the deceased about the kind of funeral wanted were known.

A majority indicated that at least the general wishes of the deceased about the kind of funeral wanted were known. But in over one-fourth of the cases, 29.7%, the wishes were unknown.

HOW MUCH INFORMATION THE DECEASED LEFT ABOUT THE KIND OF FUNERAL WANTED (FOR RESPONDENTS PERSONALLY ARRANGING A FUNERAL)

	%
General wishes were known	56.0
Left detailed information	12.7
Total first two categories	**68.7**
Wishes were not known	29.7
Don't recall	1.7

33

Detailed information was more likely to be left, however, in the case of a close friend (43.1%) or a spouse (24.0%).

9. When selecting a funeral home for their most recent funeral arrangements, almost no one contacted other homes to compare prices and services.

Almost everyone indicated they did not call or go to more than one funeral home to compare prices and services when they made their most recent funeral arrangements.

COMPARISON OF FUNERAL HOMES
(FOR RESPONDENTS PERSONALLY ARRANGING A FUNERAL)

	%
Compared	3.9
Did not compare	95.0
Don't recall	1.1

III. Attitudes Toward Preplanning

1. **A majority of people feel that they should make specific arrangements for their funerals in advance, although many feel they "probably won't get around to" such preplanning.**

Over 62% of those surveyed indicated they felt they should make prearrangements for their funerals at a funeral home, and another 9.2% indicated they had already done so. Half of the 62%, however, also indicated that they "probably won't get around to it." Another 18.9% were undecided or unconcerned about preplanning.

FEELINGS ABOUT PREARRANGING
OWN FUNERAL

	%
I already have	9.2
I feel that I should, and probably will	31.1
I feel that I should, but probably won't get around to it	30.9
Total, preceding two categories	**62.0**
It is not a good idea	10.0
Undecided or don't care	18.9

The 1974 CMA study asked a similar, although not exactly comparable, question. Of those surveyed, 54.0% agreed at least somewhat that it would be good for them to make their own funeral arrangements in advance unstead of leaving them to someone else; 24.5% disagreed at least somewhat with this; 21.4% were undecided or had no opinion. While the positive and negative answers to this question are not directly comparable to that of the current survey, a broad comparison of the results suggests that there is increased receptivity to preplanning.

Most of those who had already made prearrangements were 45 years of age or older. Attitudes toward preplanning become generally more positive as one moves west, with 16.7% of those from the West having already made arrangements versus only 4.4% of those from the East having done so.

FEELINGS ABOUT PREARRANGEMENTS

	% West	% South	% Midwest	% East
Already have	16.7	10.2	7.0	4.4
Should, and probably will	32.7	35.3	32.1	23.5
Should, but probably won't get around to it	25.6	29.5	33.0	34.2
Not a good idea	7.5	9.4	8.3	14.8
Undecided or don't care	17.4	15.6	19.5	23.2

Those with incomes of under $20,000 and who are fairly religious are slightly less positive toward preplanning than are those who have higher incomes and are less religious. (See Supplemental Table 26 for further breakdowns.)

The focus group interviews indicated that people are attracted to preplanning mainly because it makes things easier on the survivors.

"My brother-in-law died last year and he and my sister-in-law both had gone to a mortuary in Colorado and made their arrangements ahead of time. Nobody was sick or anything. But then when he died last year she said, 'You know, everything's planned.' She said after the funeral, she said, 'It really went well because,' in her grief and shock and everything, she said, 'At least I didn't have to make any important decisions.' "

"Well . . . first my father-in-law died and then two years later my mother-in-law died, and my husband and I took care of both funerals. Well, my God, what you have to go through! It's just, it's too much. And like she had bought her grave so that part was done so I figured anything that we could do, because we have five children. Anything we could do to make it easier for them we're gonna do while we're still here."

"Make it as easy as you can on the family or whoever it is. It's hard enough with the death. It's just that if you have to go door-to-door shopping trying to find a good casket or somewhere to bury them, or whatever you're going to do . . . Preparation ahead of time is nice, but unfortunately it doesn't always happen."

Some also mentioned that preplanning appealed to them because it enables a person to make "rational" purchase decisions and to control the "way" he or she "goes".

"I have this prearrangement that I did . . . I hate to say it. I was able to think rational and shop. In other words, I had a look at all the caskets and I was able to ask them the different questions . . . I thought that because of the fact that there was no real emotion involved, I was able to obtain a good price for a decent funeral."

"My plans are all made. I live being prepared. I watched some of my friends that were my age, they're no longer with us. I've got the money, I've got the time. I'd rather know that when I go, it's the way I want to go."

2. Less than half of the respondents, as well as their spouses and other family members, had made their wishes about funeral arrangements known.

In spite of the general feeling that one should preplan, over half of the respondents indicated that they, their spouses, and their parents and/or other family members had not discussed with each other the kind of funeral arrangements they wish to have.

DISCUSSION OF FUNERAL ARRANGEMENTS

	% Discussed Own Arrangements	% Discussed Spouse's Arrangements	% Discussed Parents and/or Other Family Member's Arrangements
Yes	48.2	47.8	41.8
No	51.8	52.2	58.2

There are regional differences in openness to preplanning discussions. Discussion of funeral arrangements are more likely in the West; 59.3% of those from the West had indicated their wishes to others whereas only 40.0% of those from the East had done so. Also, those who were 45 years of age or older and those who had personally arranged a funeral within the last five years were more likely to have discussed their funeral preferences than those who were younger and had had no prior arrangement experience. (See Supplemental Tables 23-25 for additional crosstabulations.)

The focus groups revealed that the failure to discuss funeral arrangements stems from the taboo nature of the topic and from an unwillingness to face up to the fact that someday one is going to die. Funeral arrangements are an easy topic to never get around to discussing.

"I think it's like religion and politics, most people just don't want to get into a discussion about it."

"But I think that's kinda one subject that people tend to shy away from. They really only discuss it when you're around the death-bed."

"People just don't want to admit that they're gonna go! You know you are, but you're not ready to sit down with somebody and say, 'Okay, I'm gonna set this whole thing up now.' You figure, 'Hell, I'm gonna be another fifty years. By then maybe they'll have everything changed,' so you don't do it."

"I guess until you get to be 65 or 70 you figure, well, you're not gonna need it. You just could be right. And if you're wrong, well, what the hell, you don't have to worry about it anyhow."

"I haven't really talked about it. I really haven't . . . My husband . . . has mentioned from time to time . . . 'If need be, I'm a veteran as you know, so you can get me buried by the government . . . ' He has mentioned it through the years . . . but he really hasn't told me any of the details of what he wants. And I haven't, I don't think I've ever mentioned to him. Maybe when we were watching that TV show, I may have said something to Tom. 'Well, you know, that cremation sounds like a

40

good idea.' But I really haven't said, 'Hey, I want you to this and such for me.' And I haven't talked to my kids about it either. I haven't talked to anyone about it. Maybe it's just my nature, because I never seem to take care of things until they're right on top of me!"

"Most people don't like to look at it. They say if you make your arrangements, you're signing your death warrant."

3. Although most of those who have discussed funeral arrangements have done so only casually, there is a segment of people who have been explicit about the details of their wishes.

The majority of respondents indicated that if they, their spouses and their other family members had previously discussed funerals, it had been only through casual comments about general arrangements. However, over one-third of those who had previously discussed arrangements were more explicit in making their wishes known.

HOW PEOPLE HAVE MADE THEIR WISHES ABOUT FUNERAL ARRANGEMENTS KNOWN

	% of Those Surveyed	% of Spouses	% of Parents and/or Other Family
Through casual comments about general funeral arrangements	56.8	59.3	54.9
Through discussion at some length of the details involved	29.7	30.4	29.0
By written instructions	7.2	4.8	7.3
Through a will	6.3	5.4	8.7

The segment made up of those who have explicitly made their wishes known through discussion at some length, written instructions or a will, consists of over 10% of the total of those surveyed.

41

% WHO HAVE EXPLICITLY MADE THEIR WISHES KNOWN

	%
Respondents	15.5
Respondents' spouses	13.6
Respondents' parents and/or other family members	10.8

People who had previously discussed funeral arrangements conveyed their preferences on two topics: whether or not to hold a funeral service and how the body should be put to rest. Many also indicated the kind of funeral service to be held.

PREFERENCES ABOUT FUNERAL ARRANGEMENTS THAT HAVE BEEN MADE KNOWN

	% Respondents	% Respondents' Spouses	% Respondents' Parents and/or Other Family
Whether or not a funeral service should be held	72.8	65.3	56.1
How the body should be put to rest (e.g., burial, cremation, etc.)	82.6	76.5	69.5
What the overall cost should be	31.5	27.8	23.8
Which funeral home should be used	37.5	32.8	35.3
Type of casket to be used	32.4	27.6	24.9
Kind of funeral service to be held	48.9	44.1	40.3

42

4. Most people would not be willing to pay for funeral arrangements before they are needed, although there is a segment that would make prepayments.

Of those who were either positive or neutral toward making pre-arrangements for their funerals, two-thirds would not be willing to make any prepayment for such prearrangements.

WILLINGNESS TO PREPAY

	%
Yes, 10% of the cost	7.4
Yes, 10% to 50%	11.1
Yes, 50% to 90%	11.5
Yes, 100%	4.7
Total willing to prepay	**34.8**
No, I would not be willing to make any prepayment	65.2

The number of people willing to make prepayments of some form is sizeable, however, and includes 34.8% of all those surveyed. And 16.2% of the respondents are willing to prepay 50% or more of the cost. (See Supplemental Table 27 for additional crosstabulations.)

Two reasons were discussed for an unwillingness to prepay: (1) a feeling that it's just something more to pay for now, and (2) concern that arrangements prepurchased might be useless and untransferrable if a person moved.

"I think that, with me, it's something extra to pay for now. You figure that, when you die, your insurance is gonna take care of your funeral. If you planned it now and wanted to pay for the whole thing, it's like buying a car or something, then it's another payment you have to make."

"Also, the majority of the reason and probably why most people don't preplan or prepay or whatever, is because of the mobilization of the American public. You don't want to go here

43

to a funeral home and say, okay, I got everything all set and I paid forty years ago. All of a sudden you're transferred to California. When you're there, you die. What, you've got to come back here? Now if this was something that would go around the United States — you have so much in a credit for your funeral and all funeral homes will go along with it — fine. You'd be buried anywhere . . ."

5. **Slightly less than a half of those surveyed were aware of funeral homes in their area offering pre-need funeral arrangements.**

There is some awareness of preplanning services. About half of the people have heard at least a little about local funeral homes that offer preplanning arrangements.

AWARENESS OF PREPLANNING
BEING OFFERED BY
AREA FUNERAL HOMES

	%
Yes, I have heard a lot about this	15.8
Yes, I have heard a little about this	31.8
Total first two categories	**47.6**
No, I have heard nothing about this	52.5

6. **Most people do not want to be contacted about prearrangement services, although a quarter of those surveyed are undecided or have no opinion about this.**

Most people do not want to be contacted about prearrangement services for themselves or their family. Only about 10% were interested in being contacted.

FEELINGS ABOUT BEING CONTACTED BY FUNERAL HOME ABOUT PREARRANGEMENTS

	For the Person Surveyed	For Their Spouse	For Their Parents and/or Other Family
I would like very much to be contacted	1.8	1.7	2.0
I wouldn't mind being contacted	10.3	9.9	8.1
I would not like to be contacted	56.3	56.8	58.5
Undecided/ no opinion	25.1	25.9	26.9
I have already been contacted	6.6	5.7	4.5

Those who were 45 or older, those with an income between $8,000 and $20,000, and those with a high school diploma or less were somewhat more receptive toward being contacted than were those who were younger, those with high incomes, or more education. (See Supplemental Tables 28-30 for specific crosstabulations.)

A few respondents in the focus groups were favorable toward being contacted or at least receiving information because it might prompt them to go ahead with preplanning.

"I think that if somebody came to the door one day and said, 'Now, we've got this here, and etc., etc., etc.,' then my husband might do it. But the thought of getting ready to go out and do it is something that he doesn't think about. It's like making a will, you kind of put that off."

"It doesn't seem like it's the easiest thing to do. I mean, if there was an ad in the paper and it said, 'Come in this week and view all the caskets and pick the one that you would like to have,' I

might even do something like that. It would be like going to the jewelry store and looking through and picking out what you want. But they never do that. They never say, 'We're open and you can come in and do this.' I think if they would advertise that maybe they would get more people in to look at the caskets and browse around. I mean, certainly it's not a pleasant thing to do but it might be something you would consider doing for a weekend. When they're done, it's done with.''

7. Most people do not have insurance designed specifically to cover funeral costs.

Only about 20% of respondents indicated that they carried insurance specifically for funeral costs.

INSURANCE SPECIFICALLY FOR FUNERAL COSTS

	% Respondents	% Respondents' Spouses	% Respondents' Parents and/or Other Family Members
Yes	20.7	19.3	19.6
No	72.6	73.9	47.8
Don't know	6.7	6.9	32.6

IV. Attitudes Toward Funeral Services

1. Most people would want a funeral service to be held for themselves and for their spouses and their parents or other family members.

More than three-quarters of those surveyed said they would prefer to have some kind of funeral service for themselves, their spouses and their parents and/or other family members.

WHETHER OR NOT A FUNERAL SERVICE SHOULD BE HELD

	For the Respondent	For the Spouse	For Parents and/or Other Family Members
Preferring a funeral service	79.0	81.7	80.8
Preferring no funeral service	11.6	9.2	5.4
Undecided or no opinion	9.4	9.1	13.8

Only 11.6% indicated they would not want a funeral service for themselves. This is much less than the 20% reported in the 1974 CMA study as stating that "when they die, they want no funeral." Actually, the 20% reported in 1974 were those who said they either "strongly agree" or "agree somewhat" with the statement, "When I die, I want no funeral." Some of those who had only "agreed somewhat" with the idea of no funeral might have preferred to have some kind of funeral service if asked to choose *between* having no funeral service and some kind of funeral service. Therefore, it is more accurate to say that 20% of those surveyed in the 1974 CMA study *agreed at least somewhat* with the idea of no funeral for themselves. This is not comparable to the current finding that 11.6% of those surveyed in 1981 would *prefer* to have no funeral service for themselves.

Geographical location and religiosity most affect people's preferences about whether or not to have a funeral service. Over one-fifth of the people in the West wanted no funeral service for themselves, whereas only 5% of those in the Midwest wanted no personal service.

% PREFERRING NO FUNERAL SERVICE FOR THEMSELVES

West	22.3
South	9.6
Midwest	5.0
East	13.6

Of those who were only slightly religious or less, 17.6% wanted no funeral service for themselves, whereas only 7.4% of those who were more religious wanted no personal funeral service. The pattern for spouses and other family members was comparable. (Supplemental Tables 31-33 provide further demographic breakdowns.)

Reasons why people feel that having a funeral service is desirable were discussed in the focus group interviews. The dominant rationale was that funeral services help the survivors to cope with their grief and to go on with living.

"Funerals are for the living . . . As far as the person that's dead, it's not gonna be that it does that person any good at all. But it certainly does the living."

"I just buried my husband about two months ago. I do think it [a funeral service] is a very good idea, because at this moment you have friends you have already forgotten for a long, long time that do come . . . You're in such a turmoil at that time, you're just glad to have somebody there with you at that time to help you out, to understand the things that are going on . . . It doesn't do anything for the person that's deceased but for the person that's living and I think that's the purpose of going."

"When people are sick you go by the hospital to see them. Now that he's dead you want to go by and pay your respects to, at

50

least to the living. I assume, maybe, you can pay it to the dead . . . It's a time for friends and a little help, you know. That's a pretty tough day to live through.

Also, a funeral service is desired because a way is needed to show respect for the deceased. Some sort of commemoration of the person's death is necessary.

"Well, I think that's the respect, by having a funeral!"

"You need some kind of commemoration in some kind of formal setting. Kind of like when you graduate, you need a little ceremony where you get your diploma. It's the same kind of, well, not a happy occasion, but you need some kind of formal service . . . It kind of marks the occasion, you know, with a ceremony . . . Otherwise it's a day like any other."

"My uncle died last year and he requested no service at all and he was cremated and it was really sad for his widow. She went ahead and respected his wishes but it was really sad because she had no, she had nobody come to her house, or there was nothing for her, you know, to give her any kind of comfort at all. She did what he wanted, but it was really bad for her and she still hasn't gotten over it."

2. **Most people prefer an "inexpensive, no frills" funeral service for themselves, but most prefer a better, more "typical" funeral service for their spouses and parents or other family members.**

Of the people who wanted some kind of funeral service to be held, the majority wanted the services for their spouses and their parents and/or other family members to be "typical" of the kind held for their family and friends. However, for themselves, the majority wanted "inexpensive, no frills" funeral services. Only a handful wanted a service that "stands out."

51

KIND OF FUNERAL SERVICE PREFERRED BY THOSE WHO WANTED A SERVICE

	For the Respondent	For the Spouse	For Parents and/or Other Family Members
A service that stands out	1.8	2.5	2.5
A funeral service typical for my family and friends	42.5	52.4	59.5
An inexpensive, no frills funeral service	55.7	45.1	38.0

There were, however, two exceptions to the general preference for the inexpensive funeral for oneself. The majority of those who had personally arranged a funeral during the past five years preferred the better, more "typical" service for themselves.

KIND OF FUNERAL SERVICE PREFERRED FOR ONESELF BY THOSE WHO WANTED A SERVICE

	% Who Had Arranged a Funeral	% Who Had Not Arranged a Funeral
A service that stands out	2.5	1.5
A funeral service typical for my family and friends	56.1	36.3
An inexpensive, no frills funeral service	41.4	62.2

A majority of people in the Midwest also preferred the better "typical" funeral service for themselves.

52

KIND OF FUNERAL SERVICE PREFERRED FOR ONESELF BY THOSE WHO WANTED A SERVICE

	% East	% Midwest	% South	% West
A service that stands out	1.2	1.4	2.9	1.6
A funeral service typical for my family and friends	37.7	51.8	38.2	38.4
An inexpensive, no frills funeral service	61.1	46.8	58.9	60.0

Several exceptions also existed to the general preference for having the better, more "typical" funeral service for one's spouse. A slight majority of those who had not arranged a funeral in the last five years preferred an inexpensive, no frills funeral service for their spouses.

KIND OF FUNERAL SERVICE PREFERRED FOR SPOUSE BY THOSE WHO WANTED A SERVICE

	% Who Had Arranged a Funeral	% Who Had Not Arranged a Funeral
A service that stands out	4.6	1.7
A funeral service typical for my family and friends	62.4	48.4
An inexpensive, no frills service	33.0	49.9

And a majority of those in the East and in the West wanted the less expensive funeral for their spouses.

53

KIND OF FUNERAL SERVICE PREFERRED FOR SPOUSE BY THOSE WHO WANTED A SERVICE

	% West	% Midwest	% South	% East
A service that stands out	2.8	3.9	1.4	2.1
A funeral service typical for my family and friends	39.4	55.3	60.1	46.9
An inexpensive, no frills funeral service	57.8	40.8	38.5	51.0

Also, slightly more of those whose incomes were lower (between $8,000 and $19,999) preferred the simpler funeral services than preferred the more typical kind for their spouses.

KIND OF FUNERAL SERVICE PREFERRED FOR SPOUSE BY THOSE WHO WANTED A SERVICE

	% Incomes $8,000 to $19,999	% Incomes $20,000 and Over
A service that stands out	2.7	2.3
A funeral service typical of my family and friends	48.5	56.4
An inexpensive, no frills service	48.8	41.3

There were no exceptions to the preference shown by the majority of all the respondents for a "typical" service for their parents and/or other family members.

Overall, those respondents who had previously arranged a funeral, and those respondents from the Midwest, showed the greatest preference for the "typical" funeral service. They differed from all the other respondents in that a greater percentage of them than in the other groups wanted the "typical" funeral service for their spouses or other family members. Also, they were the only two groups where a majority preferred the "typical" services for themselves.

Supplemental Tables 31-33 show the information from which the data in this section were derived and provide further demographic breakdowns.

3. More younger people want "typical" funeral services than do the older people.

Those respondents who were under 45 years of age showed more of a preference for "typical" funeral services than might be expected.* Although they did prefer the "no frills" service for themselves, slightly fewer of them did so than did those who were 45 years of age or older.

KIND OF FUNERAL SERVICE PREFERRED FOR ONESELF BY THOSE WHO WANTED A SERVICE

	% Under 45	% 45 or Older
Service that "stands out"	3.1	0.7
"Typical" service	44.2	41.4
"No frills" service	52.7	57.9

* *Those under 45 years of age were much more likely to have not arranged a funeral in the past five years (82%) than were those 45 years or older (68%) and those who had not arranged funerals showed less preference for the "typical" kind of funeral service. Therefore, one could expect that those under 45 would also show less of a preference for the typical service than would those 45 years of age or older.*

More of the under 45 group preferred the "typical" funeral service for their spouses than did those in the 45 and older group.

KIND OF FUNERAL SERVICE PREFERRED FOR SPOUSE BY THOSE WHO WANTED A SERVICE

	% Under 45	% 45 and Older
Service that "stands out"	3.9	1.6
"Typical" service	56.4	57.9
"No frills" service	39.8	48.6

And almost two-thirds of the younger group preferred the typical kind of service for other family members whereas only about one-half of those in the older group did so.

KIND OF FUNERAL SERVICE PREFERRED FOR PARENTS AND/OR OTHER FAMILY MEMBERS

	% Under 45	% 45 and Older
Service that "stands out"	3.7	1.3
"Typical" service	63.3	55.9
"No frills" service	33.0	42.8

Supplemental Tables 31-33 also show the breakdowns described here.

4. A "typical" funeral service is one that is reflective of a person's economic bracket, and an "inexpensive, no frills" service is one that is simple but decent, and not the cheapest possible.

Comments in the focus groups indicated that the people interested in having a funeral service "typical" of their family and friends were referring to a service expressive of their life style and station in society.

"Well, I think . . . that everybody tends to have a funeral in their wage bracket. If you're middle class, you have a middle class funeral; if you're a little wealthier, you have a better. Whatever wage bracket you're in, is the type you're gonna have. It's automatic."

"I think you're expected. If you buy under, they're gonna say, 'Well, they're really giving him a cheap.' If you buy over, it's a flashy thing. So I think it's exactly right. You have a service commensurate with your station."

"You almost have to go with an image of some type. People die and you think of the people you socialize with, of the people you know as to what type of funeral."

Those interested in having an "inexpensive, no frills" funeral service were not referring to the least expensive funeral possible, but to a "decent" funeral just a little simpler than what they believe is "typical."

"If it were mine to do, I would say I do not necessarily want the cheapest nor do I want the most expensive. I want something in between them."

"I think what it is, is what you want is something decent. Something that you don't want to think about it later on."

5. **People who want a "typical" funeral service estimate, on average, that it would cost them about $2500, whereas those who prefer a "no frills" service estimate that it would cost about $1650 and those wanting a service that "stands out" estimate it would be around $3500.**

The respondents were asked to estimate the cost of the kind of funeral service (facilities, professional services, and casket as selected) they preferred for themselves, their spouses, and their parents and/or other family members. Those who had indicated they wanted a funeral service typical for their families and friends for themselves estimated, on average, that such a funeral would cost them around $2470. Those wanting a typical funeral for their

57

spouses thought, on average, that it would cost $2480, and people wanting such a service for other family members provided an average estimate of about $2560.

AVERAGE OF THE ESTIMATES OF THE COST OF A TYPICAL FUNERAL SERVICE (FOR THOSE RESPONDENTS WANTING A TYPICAL SERVICE)

	Average of Estimates
For respondent	$2468
For respondent's spouse	$2480
For respondent's parents or other family members	$2558

The average of the estimates of the cost of no frills funeral services were about $800 to $900 less than those for typical services. People who said they preferred a no frills service for themselves thought, on average, that it would be priced at around $1670. Those wanting one for their spouses gave an average estimate of about $1610 and people wanting one for other family guessed, on average, that it would cost $1640.

AVERAGE OF THE ESTIMATES OF THE COST OF A NO FRILLS FUNERAL SERVICE (FOR THOSE RESPONDENTS WANTING A NO FRILLS SERVICE)

	Average of Estimates
For respondent	$1667
For respondent's spouse	$1608
For respondent's parents or other family members	$1640

As shown in the table below, the average of estimates by the handful of respondents who wanted services that "stand out" were about $1000 higher than the estimates for the typical service.

AVERAGE OF THE ESTIMATES OF THE COST OF A FUNERAL SERVICE THAT STANDS OUT (FOR THOSE RESPONDENTS WANTING A SERVICE THAT STANDS OUT)

	Average of Estimates
For respondent	$3429
For respondent's spouse	$3759
For respondent's parents or other family members	$3675

6. **A majority feels there should be no restrictions on who attends a funeral service, although about one-fifth do think it should be only relatives and friends.**

A majority of the respondents felt there should be no restrictions on who attends a funeral service. However, 21.6% felt there should be only relatives and friends in attendance, and another 14.9% felt this could be broadened to include acquaintances.

WHO SHOULD ATTEND A FUNERAL SERVICE

	%
No one, because there should not be a funeral service	6.7
Only immediate relatives	3.5
Relatives and friends	21.6
Relatives, friends and acquaintances	14.9
There should not be any restrictions on who attends	53.3

The finding for those indicating there should not be a funeral service is of interest because it implies that 6.7% of the respondents believe there should be no funeral service at all.* A similar question was asked in the 1974 CMA Survey, and 12.9% of the respondents indicated that, in their opinion, funerals should "be eliminated."† Although the two questions are not directly comparable, the current results suggest that there has not been a significant increase in the number of people who do not believe in funeral services.

7. **Most people feel that less than twenty minutes should be devoted to speaker's comments during a funeral service, and almost half of the people feel the comments should last no more than ten minutes.**

When asked how much total time should be devoted to speakers' comments (i.e., sermons, eulogies, and other remarks) during a funeral service, almost half of the respondents felt they should last just five to ten minutes. Most of the others indicated they should be no longer than twenty minutes in length.

TIME FOR SPEAKERS' COMMENTS

	%
Only a few minutes (5 to 10)	48.1
Several minutes (15 to 20)	35.9
Total first two categories	**84.0**
At least 30 minutes or more	5.4
Undecided or no opinion	10.6

* *The instances reported previously where respondents indicated they wanted "no funeral service" were referring to services for specific people (for themselves, their spouses or their other family members. This question, however, measures preference for no funeral service for anyone.*

† *The question was: "In your opinion, should funerals (1) Be large and involve many friends and family, (2) Stay about the same as they are now, (3) Be smaller and more private, or (4) Be eliminated?"*

8. The majority seldom or never go to the funeral of someone they know fairly well but who is not a close friend, and most seldom or never go to the funeral of an acquaintance.

When asked if they would attend the funeral service of someone whom they know fairly well but who is not a close friend, the majority (52.1%) said that they seldom or never go to such a service. One-third of those surveyed said they sometimes go, but only 14.8% said that they frequently or always attend that kind of funeral.

ATTENDANCE AT THE FUNERAL OF SOMEONE KNOWN FAIRLY WELL BUT WHO IS NOT A CLOSE FRIEND

	%		%
I always go	3.5	**Total first**	
I frequently go	11.3	**three categories**	**47.9**
Total first		I seldom go	31.4
two categories	**14.8**	I never go	20.7
I sometimes go	33.1	**Total last**	
		two categories	**52.1**

Even fewer said that they tend to go to the funeral of someone who is only an acquaintance. Over three-quarters said they seldom or never attend such a service. Only 5.1% said that they frequently or always go.

ATTENDANCE AT THE FUNERAL OF SOMEONE WHO IS ONLY AN ACQUAINTANCE

	%		%
I always go	1.2	**Total first**	
I frequently go	3.9	**three categories**	**21.3**
Total first		I seldom go	30.1
two categories	**5.1**	I never go	48.6
I sometimes go	16.2	**Total last**	
		two categories	**78.7**

61

Exceptions to this tendency to not go to the funerals of friends and acquaintances occur with different regional locations, ages, and degrees of religiosity. The majority of people in the West (58.4%) said they *do* go at least sometimes to the funeral of someone they know fairly well but not closely, whereas only one-third of those in the East said they do so, which is much less than the tendency nationwide. Those in the Midwest and South more closely follow the nationwide practice in attending this kind of funeral service.

ATTENDANCE AT THE FUNERAL OF SOMEONE KNOWN FAIRLY WELL BUT WHO IS NOT A CLOSE FRIEND

	% East	% Midwest	% South	% West
Always or frequently	9.1	14.5	16.8	18.7
Sometimes	23.2	34.0	35.4	39.7
Total first two categories	32.3	48.5	52.2	58.4
Seldom or never	67.6	51.5	47.7	41.6

Attendance at the funerals of acquaintances showed similar variations by region. Again, those in the East were less prone to attend such funerals than people in other regions.

ATTENDANCE AT THE FUNERAL OF SOMEONE WHO IS ONLY AN ACQUAINTANCE

	% East	% Midwest	% South	% West
Always or frequently	2.9	5.1	5.2	7.4
Sometimes	8.0	16.5	20.4	19.0
Total first two categories	10.9	21.6	25.6	26.4
Seldom or never	89.0	78.4	74.3	73.5

Respondents who were 45 years of age or older were more likely than usual to attend a friend's funeral, with a majority of them doing so at least sometimes. Most of those who were younger tended not to go to such funerals.

ATTENDANCE AT THE FUNERAL OF SOMEONE KNOWN FAIRLY WELL BUT WHO IS NOT A CLOSE FRIEND

	% Under 45	% 45 or Older
Always or frequently	9.3	19.0
Sometimes	30.3	35.8
Total first two categories	39.6	54.8
Seldom or never	60.4	45.2

The same variations by age were true for attendance at funerals for acquaintances.

People who were rather religious were also more likely than usual to attend funerals for friends. A majority of them said they go to such funerals at least sometimes, whereas only 38.4% of those who were less religious said that they do so.

ATTENDANCE AT THE FUNERAL OF SOMEONE KNOWN FAIRLY WELL BUT WHO IS NOT A CLOSE FRIEND

	% Rather Religious	% Not Very Religious
Always or frequently	18.0	10.2
Sometimes	36.6	28.2
Total first two categories	54.6	38.4
Seldom or never	45.4	61.6

The same variations by religiosity held for attendance at funerals for acquaintances. Supplemental Tables 36 and 37 provide additional demographic breakdowns.

63

9. More people go to the wake, visitation or calling hours of someone they know fairly well and of an acquaintance than go to the funerals for such people.

Almost two-thirds of those surveyed said that they go at least sometimes to the visitation, calling hours or wake of someone they know fairly well but who is not a close friend. Almost twice as many said they frequently or always attend such obervances (28.2%) as said they frequently or always attend the funeral for such a person (14.8%).

ATTENDANCE AT THE WAKE OR VISITATION/CALLING HOURS FOR SOMEONE KNOWN FAIRLY WELL BUT WHO IS NOT A CLOSE FRIEND

	%		%
I always go	7.6	**Total first**	
I frequently go	20.6	**three categories**	**64.1**
Total first		I seldom go	21.2
two categories	**28.2**	I never go	14.7
I sometimes go	35.9	**Total last**	
		two categories	**35.9**

Just under 40% of those surveyed said that they at least sometimes attend the wake, visitation or calling hours of someone who is just an acquaintance, which is almost twice as many as said they attend such a person's funeral at least sometimes (21.4%).

ATTENDANCE AT THE WAKE OR VISITATION/CALLING HOURS OF SOMEONE WHO IS JUST AN ACQUAINTANCE

	%		%
I always go	4.0	**Total first**	
I frequently go	7.5	**three categories**	**39.9**
Total first		I seldom go	25.8
two categories	**11.5**	I never go	34.3
I sometimes go	28.4	**Total last**	
		two categories	**60.1**

Comments made in the focus group interviews shed some light on the reasons for the greater tendency to attend wakes or visitation/calling hours than to attend funeral services. Wakes, visitation and calling hours are viewed as being invaluable to the family of the deceased in helping them get through the initial period after the death of their loved one. Such an occasion provides family members with necessary companionship and support.

"They come, they sit, they talk about old times, or they try to make the other person forget about what just happened. It just keeps them company. They feel better. They're not alone."

"When you're alone you have the tendency to just sit and dwell on it. It gets you down more than trying to get over the situation."

Attendance also helps ease people's grief because pleasant memories of the departed person are discussed.

"You cry . . . you think about the good times, and everybody says, 'Well, we'll see you next week' or 'We'll go on'. You always go on. It's just that you try to get over the hurt . . . The more family you have or the more friends, the more good things that you hear about the people that passed away, the better off you feel. So it doesn't hurt as much."

"What it does for you is that nobody has ever come up and said, 'I'm glad that bastard's dead.' Everybody says something nice. It's kinda a nice thing if you're the one that's had the loss."

"It's great to have the people come to the wake because you're there and at least you can look at the person who died and you know it brings your memories. It helps, it really does."

There was a general feeling therefore that one should go to wakes, visitation and calling hours so as not to deprive the bereaved of this assistance. Some even felt a social obligation to attend.

"Just imagine yourself with a member of your family dead and no one does come. How would you feel then? . . . I certainly would go, whether it's a wake with food and booze or a chapel,

65

wherever it may be. Your neighbor, certainly, would have come and paid his respects to the family . . . I'd do it and expect the same from you. If you didn't, ah . . ."

Also, some felt that attendance at the wake or visitation/calling hours was a good way to honor the deceased person by giving him " good send off." One man talked about this when he explained why he wanted a wake for himself.

"Because I believe in it. I'm Irish and I believe in a good send-off. They sat up there and had a party when I come into this world, and I want them to have one when I go out of this world."

Attendance at wakes, visitation or calling hours has a lighter side as well, in that it is an opportunity to see and socialize with old friends.

"A lot of people even mention, you know, the comment is made, 'Hey, I haven't seen you for years. We always seem to meet at weddings and funerals . . .' In some ways the wake is kind of a get-together of long-lost friends or something like that."

"You meet a lot of people there, who you haven't seen in years, and you can go out and have a drink afterwards."

10. **Most people think the combined visitation, calling hours or wake and the funeral service should be in total a period of no more than two days.**

The respondents were asked how many days, in all, the visitation calling or wake period *and* the funeral service should take, not counting the time between the visitation period and funeral service. Over three-fourths indicated they thought it should take two days. Only 21.7% thought it should last three or more days, which is the period needed for the wake or visitation to last the traditional two or more nights.

NUMBER OF DAYS THE VISITATION, CALLING OR WAKE PERIOD AND THE FUNERAL SERVICE SHOULD TAKE

	%		%
1 day	37.2	3 days	20.7
2 days	41.1	4 or more	1.0
Total 1 or 2 days	**78.3**	**Total 3 or more days**	**21.7**

Those in the West showed even more of an interest in keeping the duration of the whole period to one day, with almost half of them opting for it, and Easterners also favored one day slightly more than two. Southerners had the largest proportion of any other group favoring a two-day period. More of the Midwesterners favored three or more days than did those in any of the other regional groups.

TOTAL DURATION OF THE WAKE/ VISITATION AND FUNERAL PERIOD

	% EAST	% MIDWEST	% SOUTH	% WEST
1 day	41.4	31.1	33.6	47.8
2 days	36.5	43.9	48.6	30.4
3 days	20.9	23.4	17.3	21.0
4 or more	1.2	1.6	0.5	0.8

Those who were rather religious, had more education (some college or more) or had a higher income ($20,000 or more) also had a slightly larger proportion favoring a one-day period over the other durations. The breakdowns for all three groupings are quite similar, so only the figures for the differences by religiosity are cited below. The other breakdowns are shown in Supplemental Table 35.

67

TOTAL DURATION OF THE WAKE/ VISITATION AND FUNERAL PERIOD

	% Rather Religious	% Not Very Religious
1 day	34.3	42.0
2 days	42.3	39.5
3 days	22.1	17.8
4 or more	1.3	0.7

That quarter of all the people surveyed who had previously arranged a funeral showed more of a preference for the traditional funeral/wake period than the other people, with 26.0% of them favoring three or more days.

TOTAL DURATION OF THE WAKE/ VISITATION AND FUNERAL PERIOD

	% Who Have Arranged a Funeral	% Who Have Not Arranged a Funeral
1 day	31.7	39.6
2 days	42.3	40.6
3 days	25.3	18.6
4 days or more	0.7	1.2

The reason people preferred a shorter wake, visitation or calling period, and consequently a shorter total funeral/wake-visitation period, was that it would lessen the emotional and physical strain on the surviving relatives.

"It seems to me that having two or three nights is such a tremendous emotional strain on the family. My mother-in-law

68

passed away last year and they only had the wake one night and the funeral home was packed, just jammed. Then they had the funeral the next morning around ten or eleven. There were quite a few there then but not as many as the night before. I don't think any of us could have stood another night of that. Because everyone was telling what a great person she was, you know and always talking about her. And we loved her dearly. But, you know, it just got to the point, that you just thought, 'Well, if one more person says something I'm just going to break down and scream!' And when I left there, I was just shaking! And I couldn't have taken another night, and she was only my mother-in-law!"

"When my grandmother passed away, we had [the wake] the two nights and then the following morning the funeral. The first night we went, there were a lot of people and everything and it was very emotional. Then after we got home and during the course of the following day my mother kind of settled down a little bit. As it got closer to the time when she had to go back to the funeral home . . . she just got so tensed up and said, 'I wish I didn't have to go a second night.' You know, just to get the funeral and get it over with. I even found myself, it was very traumatic as far as the emotional aspect of having to go again and sit there for another full evening of four hours, or whatever. I think it should be shortened to just one night."

"When my father-in-law died, my mother-in-law wanted that type of thing. We got there at 10:00 in the morning and left there at 11:00 at night, two straight days, and the third day of course was the funeral. By the end of the funeral we were ready to say, 'George, move over. There's room for three or four more in that box.' We were all just totally wiped out, emotionally drained and physically wiped out. I think that is just a bummer. I would never allow that."

11. **Most people preferred that the casket be open during at least some portion of the visitation, calling hours or wake and funeral period.**

When asked about what arrangements they preferred for viewing

69

the remains, 60.7% of those surveyed indicated they preferred that the casket be open during at least part of the whole funeral/wake or visitation period. About one-fourth of all the respondents wanted an open casket both during the visitation/wake and the funeral, whereas more, 37.2%, wanted an open casket only during the visitation/wake hours. Another 14.2% wanted the casket present at these ceremonies, but closed the whole time. Over a tenth wanted the casket to not be present at all.

PREFERENCE FOR VIEWING ARRANGEMENTS

	%
Have the casket open during the visitation/ calling hours/wake and during the funeral	23.5
Have the casket open during the visitation/ calling hours/wake but closed during the funeral	37.2
Total first two categories	**60.7**
Have the casket closed during the visitation/ calling hours/wake and the funeral	14.2
Not have the casket present at all	11.4
Undecided or no opinion	13.8

The same question was asked in the 1974 CMA Survey, but the option of selecting "undecided or no opinion" was not given. Although this lessens the comparability of those results to the current ones, some shifts in preferences are suggested from the following table, which shows the 1981 results (recalculated without the undecided segment) compared to the 1974 results.

70

PREFERENCE FOR VIEWING ARRANGEMENTS

	% 1974	% 1981	% Change
Casket open during the visitation/calling hours/wake and during the funeral	30.5	27.3	− 3.2
Casket open only during the visitation/calling hours/wake	51.6	43.0	− 8.6
Closed casket	13.1	16.5	+ 3.4
No casket*	4.8	13.2	+ 8.4

There appears to be an increase in the number of people not wanting the casket present at all and a decrease in preference for an open casket.

In the current survey, regional differences provided exceptions to these findings, with those in the West far less interested in open caskets. Less than half of the Westerners (43.6%) wanted the casket open at any point, and a quarter of them wanted no casket present at all. The Midwesterners were just the opposite, with more than was usual wanting some kind of open casket (71.1%) and fewer than usual wanting no casket (6.0%).

PREFERENCE FOR VIEWING ARRANGEMENTS

	% East	% Midwest	% South	% West
Open casket	57.0	71.1	64.3	43.6
Closed casket	15.4	11.5	15.1	15.5
No casket	11.4	6.0	8.3	24.5
Undecided/no opinion	16.3	11.3	12.4	16.5

* *This option in the 1974 CMA Study was actually worded, "Have the body not present during calling hours or the funeral."*

Educational differences also had some effect on viewing preferences. Almost three-fourths of those with a high school or less education preferred some kind of open casket, whereas only half of those with more education wanted an open casket. Those with higher education were twice as likely to want a closed casket or no casket as did those with less education.

PREFERENCE FOR VIEWING ARRANGEMENTS

	% High School or Less	% Some College or More
Open casket	72.0	50.8
Closed casket	9.0	19.0
No casket	7.1	15.3
Undecided/no opinion	12.0	14.9

Experience in arranging funerals produced similar differences in preferences about viewing, with those with prior arrangement experience being more favorable toward open caskets.

PREFERENCE FOR VIEWING ARRANGEMENTS

	% Who Have Arranged a Funeral	% Who Have Not Arranged a Funeral
Open casket	71.4	56.1
Closed casket	10.6	15.8
No casket	9.0	12.4
Undecided/no opinion	9.0	15.8

Those who were rather religious, had lower incomes, or were 45 years or older also were more favorable toward an open casket than those who were less religious, had higher incomes or were younger. The breakdowns for these three groupings are similar, so only those for religiosity are shown below. The other breakdowns may be found

72

in Supplemental Table 34.

PREFERENCE FOR VIEWING ARRANGEMENTS

	% Rather Religious	% Not Very Religious
Open casket	64.7	54.7
Closed casket	14.7	13.8
No casket	9.5	14.0
Undecided/no opinion	11.2	17.4

Several reasons were mentioned in the focus groups for people's preferences for either an open or closed casket. Those who wanted to be able to view the body felt that it makes the death real and helps one accept the fact that the person is gone.

"I think that also helped, because it doesn't seem real, you know, when you lose somebody that you love, and you can't imagine that they're really dead, you know. And until you — I know myself — until I saw them in the casket it just wasn't real."

"I didn't see my husband . . . He came back from Viet Nam [in a closed casket] and I didn't know and I didn't see him. It took me a long time before I could really handle it. Was that really him or not? When my baby died, I saw it . . . so for me it was helpful. I mean it wasn't a pleasant thing to look at a dead body, but it was something that was helpful."

"It finalizes it, I think. Finalization, it's the final realization that he's gone, he's dead. You accept it and you go ahead and do what you have to do."

Some liked an open casket because they found it comforting to see the deceased looking peaceful, and, in some cases, better than when alive.

"A person, especially those that have cancer, who suffers so

73

terribly much and then when they do put them in a casket, they do look beautiful. They don't look like you saw them suffering. They look very peaceful and very well made up, even though they lose a lot of weight or they suffer. They still look a lot better than when they were alive. I think that's a consolation to see somebody looking that good, especially if somebody suffered quite a bit."

Most of those who were against the viewing of the body felt that no matter how much of an effort is made to prepare the body, it never "looks natural." They preferred to remember the departed based on their memory of the person.

"I don't really care for it myself. I like to remember them as they were. And usually they're, I don't care how nice they make them look and what have you, they never look the same, you know. They're dead! There's no life, and they may make them look nice but not like when they were alive."

"When I viewed the body, my mother, well for one thing the past year she was terribly, terribly thin because of her illness so she wasn't . . . for the whole past year . . . of her life, she was extremely different from the way I'd known her since childhood . . . She was a person who never wore any make up, of any kind. And then she was made up in the coffin so that didn't look right. As you say, I could recognize her. I knew it was she, but it didn't look real. I don't think there's any pleasure, either, in viewing the body in the coffin. The only thing, I think of my mother saying, 'You should check to make sure,' I guess, that they're there, or something."

A few respondents said that they preferred the atmosphere of ceremonies with closed caskets. There is less emotional strain associated with a closed casket.

"I have found that 90% of all the funerals that I went to were open coffin. When my wife's father died, we had a closed coffin, because it was just the circumstances. And I found the atmosphere of the funeral completely different than when you have an open coffin. It's not so much, 'Well, I knew him when.' It's more distant, okay? And more realistic. The emotion is

not stimulated. So somebody walks up and they see him and all of a sudden they burst into tears or whatever. The casket's closed. Naturally everybody inquires why. But it's more subdued. You're not open to a lot of emotional outbursts or something that you don't expect. After that experience my wife and I decided if it was I, or my wife, or my family, we would have a closed coffin."

V. Attitudes Toward Funeral Homes and Funeral Directors

. Most people have a preferred funeral home, and consider it to be good to excellent.

When asked if they had a "preferred funeral home" that they ould probably turn to if needed, 61.6% of all of the people sureyed said that they did.

DO YOU HAVE A
PREFERRED FUNERAL HOME?

	%
Yes	61.6
No	38.4

As might be expected, a larger proportion of those who had rranged a funeral during the last five years had a preferred funeral ome than those without such experience. However, over half of ose who had not had recent experience making arrangements at funeral home still indicated that they had a preferred funeral home.

DO YOU HAVE A PREFERRED FUNERAL HOME?

	% Who Have Arranged a Funeral	% Who Have Not Arranged a Funeral
Yes	77.8	54.7
No	22.2	45.3

Age and regional differences also affected whether or not people ad a certain funeral home they would turn to in time of need. lmost three-fourths of those who were older (45 years of age and ore) said they had a preferred home. People who were under 45 ears of age, however, provided an exception to the general tendency ɔ prefer a certain home. A majority of them did *not* have one,

79

and only 46.0% said they had a preferred funeral home.

DO YOU HAVE A PREFERRED FUNERAL HOME?

	% Under 45 Years	% 45 Years and Over
Yes	46.0	72.5
No	54.0	27.5

Respondents in the West also provided an exception, with a majority of them not having a preferred firm and only 48.0% of them saying they did have one.

DO YOU HAVE A PREFERRED FUNERAL HOME

	% East	% Midwest	% South	% West
Yes	61.2	66.8	65.6	48.0
No	38.8	33.2	34.4	52.0

Differences in religiosity, education and sex also had some impact on whether or not respondents had preferred funeral homes. Male and those who were not very religious, or had less education, had a smaller percentage who said they preferred a certain home than did females or those who were rather religious or had more education. The proportions for all three groupings are similar, so only those for differences in religiosity are shown below. The other results may be found in Supplemental Table 38.

DO YOU HAVE A PREFERRED FUNERAL HOME?

	% Rather Religious	% Not Very Religious
Yes	66.7	54.5
No	33.3	45.5

Discussion in the focus groups indicated that a person who had a preferred funeral home that he would go to in time of need considered it, in a very personal sense, to be "my" funeral home.

"We're from Chicago and all of my family has gone to one funeral home and that's the one we always go back to. And we had a son who passed away three years ago and, no questions about it, that's where we went. Because we know the care that they give us. And they're friends, really."

"Twelve years ago I lost my wife, we were married 33 years. Well, we went back to Chicago and everybody, my folks were buried by an undertaker and my in-laws and so on and so forth. And so it was sort of a family deal and we consider the place our place."

Often people talked about funeral directors in the same sense, and thought about them as their funeral directors. This is shown in the following dialogue in which one man asked another if he too had his "own" undertaker.

"Did you go to the first undertaker? Was your undertaker, your undertaker, like I felt at one time?"

"Well, the undertaker that I . . ."

"I mean, well, did you, you wouldn't of went anyplace else. I mean, this was your man, right?"

"Well, this was my man because he was involved with me in Boy Scouts."

Of those respondents who said that they had a preferred funeral home, 55.3% rated it as excellent, meaning it was "satisfactory in every way." Just about all the rest (43.0% of the total) said their funeral home was good, meaning "generally satisfactory." Only 15 people (1.6%) felt their home was just fair, meaning "generally satisfactory, but some things are not good," and none rated their preferred funeral homes as falling into the categories of either "poor" or "bad."

RATING OF PREFERRED FUNERAL HOME

	%
Excellent — satisfactory in every way	55.3
Good — generally satisfactory	43.0
Total first two categories	**98.3**
Fair — generally satisfactory, but some things are not good	1.6
Poor — not satisfactory on several important things	0.0
Bad — very unsatisfactory	0.0

Demographic differences among the respondents did not produce any major exceptions to or variations on these ratings, although people 45 years of age or older were slightly more likely to choose the excellent rating than were those younger. Supplemental Table 39 shows the demographic breakdowns.

Although it is to be expected that any funeral home a person selects as his preferred place to turn to when necessary would have to be regarded in a positive way by that individual, the high ratings given by those surveyed to these homes, coupled with the large percentage of the total group who had preferred funeral homes, indicates that most people are generally satisfied with the funeral services to which they have access.

These results are similar to those of the 1974 CMA Study, where respondents were asked to rate the funeral home they "knew most about" using exactly the same categories.

1974 RATING OF FUNERAL
HOME KNOWN MOST ABOUT

	%
Excellent	50.4
Good	41.2
Fair	6.8
Poor	1.3
Bad	0.3

82

Although these earlier ratings were slightly less positive than the current ones, the difference is most likely not due to an increase in positive attitudes toward funeral services, but to the fact that the funeral homes rated in 1974 were only ones that the respondents were familiar with and not ones they had come to consider as "their own."

2. The funeral director is regarded as the key to satisfactory funerary services, and people expect him and his staff to be, above all else, constantly attentive, caring and supportive.

Comments in the focus groups indicated that people tend to think of the funeral home as synonymous with the funeral director. For example, they tended to refer to a good relationship with a funeral home in terms of a good relationship with the funeral director(s).

" . . . we know the care that they gave us and they're friends, really."

" . . . you wouldn't of went anyplace else. I mean, this was your man, right?"

People feel that the funeral director performs a much needed service, and how he performs it can greatly affect how satisfactory they find services of the funeral home to be.

"But the funeral director makes all the difference in the world."

"It's a terrible job and somebody has to do it. But you get used to everything."

"Like a doctor. I couldn't cut into someone, but thank God someone can."

They have definite expectations of what services the funeral director should provide to them. Most importantly, they want the funeral director to coordinate and carry out all the practical arrangements for properly putting the deceased to rest, because they would not want to or be able to do so themselves due to grief and lack of knowledge of what to do.

83

"I think . . . If death does come to the house, and someone like myself who doesn't have anything prepared as far as a plot or anything, the funeral director would then come in very handy for the survivors. He would then take care of the arrangements . . . he would take care of the cemetery and explain, you know. From that standpoint it would be good . . . He takes a lot of it. You don't have time to think in a lot of cases, especially if it's a very sudden shock. He'll just, 'Well, don't worry about it, we'll take care of this, you know, and I'll call you,' and everything's taken care of. And I think at that point, you're paying for a service and you should be getting a service."

"Usually, your funeral director will lay out the flowers for you unless, you know, you want to buy your own. If you get a good funeral director . . . everything should run pretty smooth, because, I mean, he's catching you in a state of shock, the whole family's in turmoil."

Many told of how they had relied on the funeral director's guidance in deciding what to buy. Those who considered the guidance to have been honest felt it was of real service to them.

"My stepfather passed away two years ago and my mother wanted a funeral for him and viewing, but she wanted him cremated afterwards. The mortuary was really good in that and went the opposite way. When we were looking at caskets, he steered us really to the cheapest one and he said, 'If he's going to be cremated afterwards, why put the extra expenses on a fancy casket?' And this was really nice. It was gray cloth on the outside, and had satin on the inside . . . I don't think really anybody ever knew the difference. It had a flag over the thing because he was a veteran. So we really appreciated that, that he wasn't playing on anybody's grief, and gave us the cheapest casket they had. He said, 'This is gonna be burned up anyway.'"

"It depends on your funeral director, too, because he can kinda lead you. We just buried my dad in September, and this one was super! He said, 'You don't need, you know, a $20,000 casket. This is fine, and this is in your price range,' and you know, blah, blah, blah. And the same with the cement thing. 'You don't

need this! This one is waterproof and this one isn't, but, you know, it doesn't make any difference anyway.' "

Some also look to the funeral director to help them and other family members handle their grief in a socially acceptable way at difficult points during the ceremonies.

"They themselves are equipped to handle that. Going through this emotional thing with other families on a day-to-day basis they know how to . . . calm nerves with a tranquilizer, or smelling salts or something. But if you're just with something like a friend, hell, they aren't gonna carry smelling salts or something to help you along the way. I think there's a comforting there."

In general, people think of the funeral director as the expert they can turn to, to get them through all the complicated details and pressures of a most unpleasant and traumatic period. A few were also interested in the funeral director making this expertise available to them for a longer period of time in the form of financial counseling.

"They also supplied the gentleman that comes around, let's see, he comes around every month, up until the time all my sister's insurance, pension programs, and so on and so forth are taken care of. He gives her semi-legal advice. He can't be a direct lawyer. But he does guide her. And that's all included in the package price of the funeral which was kind of nice because she lives on the far South Side and I live out here and, you know, the driving back and forth can get to be a pain."

"I would like to say one thing, I think all the funeral homes should have what this one on the South Side had. And that's a man available to talk to who can help you with insurance, pension programs, whatever is involved. It might not be so necessary if the woman dies, but when the man dies, you've probably got retirement programs here or there, you might have insurance policies that just kinda have been put in the vault and forgotten about or God knows what else. To have a guy that can track that down is very, very nice."

People also have definite expectations of how the funeral director

85

and his staff should act. People expect them to be "caring" and "supportive," and want to feel that they're "trying to do their best for you." Several mentioned that, although they knew that funeral directors and staff were human "like anybody else," they still expected them to be courteous, attentive and caring at all times because of the sensitive and serious nature of the services that they provide. These were admitted to be high standards, but people said they cannot tolerate the funeral staff falling short of them. This is evidenced in the following comments by two men, one of whom had an unsatisfactory encounter with a funeral staff member.

"Well, I had that feeling . . . when a funeral director was assigned my shift. He was really nonpersonal. I went in there, actually up to the [head] funeral director and requested another staff assistant because he was kind of abrupt with a lot of people and everything else. I said, hey, this is no way to run this shop."

"I would say, unfortunately, he mighta had a bad day, too, like anybody else. But unlike most companies where you just walk into the company and sometime during the day you can have, you know, a good laugh session on what's going on, whereas this person, whenever he's there, you can't . . . It can get outta hand that way. But if it was a very serious funeral, and you kinda have the caretaker in the office laughing and giggling around . . . So it's somewhat of a show business-type thing where they have to also always maintain a reverence-type thing because they don't know what is the situation or what could develop. And they also have to have the experience if something does get out of hand . . . to know how to handle it . . . They have to always have a professional image. It's not, 'Today, I don't care . . . I can be kinda lackadaisacal,' or 'I'm in a bad mood, I don't care what these people say,' because they don't know what could develop."

Another aspect of the high expectations people have of how funeral personnel should act, is their feeling that a funeral director and establishment should provide prompt and willing service, even during holiday periods. Failure to do so produces great displeasure.

"My cousin died on Good Friday. The guy [the funeral director] was all bent outta shape . . . he was real bent outta shape.

86

And they didn't 'wake' him until after Easter Sunday."

"I lost a brother three years ago, and the funeral director that we had always gone to, that the family in the neighborhood had always used, it happened to be the 4th of July, and he wasn't around. And he had a partner, so to speak, that would handle it. So my sister-in-law approached the funeral director. He was very put out, so to speak, that my brother didn't die more conveniently. It was a holiday, you know. 'Where you gonna get a doctor, lawyer, undertaker, on a holiday?' That was his attitude. The regular fellow took over and everything was very pleasant after that, but it was a very bad, a very distasteful experience, to say the least."

3. **People feel that the funeral director has a great deal of power over them, and, like a car salesman, is in a position to manipulate and take advantage of them.**

Although people in the focus groups were, on the whole, satisfied with their own experiences with funerary services, there was a feeling that the average funeral director is in a position to take advantage of his customers. Much of this feeling stemmed from an overall impression of the funeral industry as a "mystery business" in which much of the activities and costs are hidden from public view. The average person was seen as having no way of knowing whether or not he was being "ripped off," whether he is or not.

"You've got a cross section of society like you do with any group there, right? And one thing that I think we've pretty much established here is that their ability to abuse is very high. Whether they do or not is a separate issue, but their ability, because they get no visibility. They have very little visibility. People, their quote 'customers,' are at their lowest resistance level, from a marketing standpoint, and there's no competition in the industry. Most people go to one place and even if you knew nobody and somebody died, are you gonna shop around? So they don't have all the classic business-type things. And so therefore, I think that's where it comes from . . . For all you know the person you have, whoever it is, that you think very good of might be the greatest abuser in the place. But he's covered it up well, you know . . ."

"It's a mystery business, for sure. We as lay persons, we know less . . . I know less of the funeral business than I know of a doctor or medical. Because you're there and so forth. These are mystery people. They can put you to sleep financially real fast."

Additional concern about the funeral director came from the perception that people in need of funeral services are in a state of grief which makes them vulnerable to being manipulated.

" . . . their quote 'customers' are at their lowest resistance level, from a marketing standpoint . . . "

Finally, the motivations of the funeral director were suspect in some people's minds because, due to the nature of his business, he profits from other people's tragedies.

"You know what makes me nervous about anybody . . . you see they're making a living on other people's tragedies. And they're . . . you know, it's just terrible, because they're sitting around waiting for people to die. That feeds their families."

The perceived lack of information about funeral costs and operations as well as the perception that the funeral director earns his living from interacting with people who are in an unnatural, vulnerable state of mind created the general feeling among the people in the focus groups that funeral directors have great power over their customers and can easily take advantage of them. While people do not think of their own funeral directors in this way, many feel that some funeral directors do take advantage of their position of power to "milk" their customers. There is a feeling that this must be so given the position funeral directors are in.

"The bottom line is the buck, just like you said, it is *the buck."*

"Mostly in the area of caskets they catch people at a very inopportune time and take advantage of them."

"I had an experience about three weeks ago, a super deluxe funeral, if you want to spend about $40,000. The more money you spend, the better funeral you get. It's strictly dollars and

cents. They show you a casket for $2,000, they show you a casket for $8,000. Then they show you the concrete vault . . . it ranges from $94 to I think it was $15,000. Everything is progressive. The better stuff you want. They just put it on the tab and you pay after the funeral . . . Then you have to have the [cemetery] lot opened. That costs you a damned good amount, even if you own the lot. So by the time they've worked you over, they have took a pretty good cut out of you."

"Then you go into a place and the guy takes a look at you and if you're wearing a diamond or what have you, he figures, uhhhh, yeh. And he's gonna sock it to you."

In every one of the five focus groups, the position of the funeral director was likened by some to a car salesman. The following description by one man of his experience in arranging a funeral typifies the attitudes of people who drew such a comparison.

"I helped bury my father-in-law. I went with my brother-in-law to the funeral home. He was in no condition to be making any decisions. I sell cars for a living and dealing with the undertaker is just like dealing with an automobile salesman. They have a beautiful routine. He sat us down in the office first. He asked all those qualifying questions so he could find out what we could afford. Naturally there was no prices on anything, he quoted prices . . . But I never bothered to dicker with the man and I know I could . . . They have a beautiful routine . . . and naturally the guilt plays in there a little bit. The man knew that I was the son-in-law and that my brother-in-law was the son, so naturally he leaned towards him to lay the guilt in a little. You know, 'Would your father want it this way?' "

Beyond their concern over the funeral director's position, several people also worried about the possibility that funeral directors may not act in good faith in those areas where the customer does not actually see the results of the services performed.

"Every once in a while it comes up in the paper about funeral directors. You keep hearing about you can't bury her with her diamond ring because you don't know if it will go into the

89

ground . . . and now with gold teeth, I mean, I hate to sound morbid. But it's not a Mickey Mouse type deal any more. It's a lot of money. Then it might just hang on the fact that the reputation of the funeral director, which sometimes, you wouldn't even question. But you see that once in a while and you keep thinking how much money that could be. That could be a lot of money."

"Since you brought that up, if there are degrees of preservation and I would elect a much advanced thing, how do I know I got it? . . . If the public sits here and believes that since they handle our dead they're all lily white . . . that's naive. Same as attorneys and doctors, preachers."

"Well, you wonder, I mean sometimes you wonder, do they put, you know, I mean it's a nice casket, you pay for it. I just wonder, maybe, do they take that casket back and . . . and maybe put it in a box. I mean, you don't know what they put it in if you don't see them lower it."

"They work them over pretty good . . . another couple, both are undertakers . . . Some of the stories he told me I wouldn't repeat to you because what they do to those bodies is sinful . . . no respect for the body. Mutilation of those bodies. Maliciously and then at Christmas time they decorate the bodies in a disrespectful way. It's just deplorable. As a matter of fact he told me that if you permit an autopsy, you're crazy. I don't agree with that. But if you permit an autopsy, to these people, they just hack a body open and go into the organ of suspect and just leave it . . . That's why, for my part of this conversation, from soup to nuts, from the florist to the embalming schools, it needs a lot of regulation . . . But when they just rip them open like a damn chicken! . . . That's very routine, obviously, for those people. Much as making coffee at home."

It is important to note, however, that the public sees only the opportunity for unethical behavior, and therefore the likelihood of such behavior. For the most part, they do not associate such behavior with their own funeral home.

4. People feel that they have to rely almost completely on the the integrity of the funeral director to assure honest service and therefore turn to the recommendations of relatives and close friends when selecting one.

Because funeral directors were felt to be in a position to take advantage of their customers, people felt that it is only the director's degree of integrity which determines whether he does so or not. Consequently, people want a funeral director in whom they can feel a strong sense of trust. It is only this trust that can ensure honest service.

"I would say that a lot of times people go in there and they really can't afford it. And because of their emotional state they're really being taken advantage of . . . and they haven't got time to shop around. Somebody just passes away and they know somebody, they're in the area . . . they're relying upon his integrity to be honest with them."

"I think that's the key issue though. The business of the integrity, the perceived integrity."

"Just like doctors, some doctors will take everything you can get, and others are more personable."

Although people felt the potential for abuse is high in the funeral industry, most people in the focus groups, as already noted, thought that most funeral homes and directors are relatively honest because, they reason, word would get around if they were not. The dishonest firm would eventually go out of business.

"I would say probably most funeral homes are fair to a degree, because if they weren't, after six months people would start thinking, well, you know, because they talk about it amongst themselves. If enough people got together in the community and said, well, this guy's really making a buck, you wouldn't be making it anymore."

"If somebody's ripping someone off, chances are you're not gonna get someone referring them to you. And that's why I don't think there's much of that going on."

"I think, like any other business, if you don't do a good job, you're outta business."

People, therefore, rely heavily on word-of-mouth information, particularly the recommendations of relatives and trusted friends, when selecting which funeral home and director to use.

"Well, they [funeral homes] have to be nice. I mean that's their business . . . If you hear from this family or from that family, 'Oh, he was very nice over there,' well, 'We'll go back over there with the rest.' And the kids and their kids go, and it keeps on like that."

"But before I looked in the yellow pages I'd call some friends. And it's the word of mouth, it's the image they have established for themselves."

"I think what you should do is go to someone, either that someone in the family has or a close friend has, you know, that you can ask them about it. But just, you know, to go through the phone book and just pick one because it's right on the corner close to your house, I mean, that don't work."

The primacy of word-of-mouth information as a factor in deciding on a funeral home was confirmed in the survey results. Respondents were asked to rank in order of importance five factors influencing their selection of a funeral home. The two factors ranked highest both centered on word-of-mouth information. "Prior experience with the funeral home by oneself, family and friends" received an average ranking of 1.98 and the "funeral director's reputation in the community" received an average ranking of 2.80. Although both are important, information from family and friends is clearly given precedence over information from others.

IMPORTANCE OF FACTORS IN
SELECTING A FUNERAL HOME

	Average Ranking
Prior experience with the funeral home by oneself, family or friends	1.98
Funeral director's reputation in the community	2.80
Appearance and "feeling" of the funeral home and staff	2.84
Convenience of the funeral home to one's home	3.34
Ethnic or religious affiliation of the funeral home	4.00

"Appearance and 'feeling' of the funeral home and staff" was ranked a close third at 2.84, which lends support to the finding from the focus groups reported earlier that people have high expectations about the tone set by the funeral staff.

The preference for using the recommendations of family and friends when selecting a funeral home was reflected in the anxiety expressed by several focus group participants who had recently moved to their current locales. They worried about how they would go about selecting a home without having family or trusted friends in the area to advise them.

"One thing came to my mind, going to the funeral of a friend. How do you know who to go to when there's a death in the family? Because they were not pleased at all with their situation. They found it horrible, really. It was a bad situation. How do you know where to go, what do you do? That's a problem that I perceive, if you're new in the area and don't know who to go to."

"I've never had an experience with having to make any kind of arrangement, and I don't even know what I would do. I guess the first thing that I would do would be to call somebody that had an experience or go to the yellow pages . . . I'm not from around here. My family's not around here . . ."

"My wife and I have not had any intimate family relationships with funerals for many, many years. Obviously, the relationships that we have, or the information that we have had has been the result of publications, etc., the feelings about funeral directors, and some of the information that comes over the newspaper, which may or may not be correct. Nevertheless, going back to the point before, you feel somewhat helpless. It isn't like going to buy a television where you kinda have a feeling about a Sony or Motorola or the quality or what you're buying or what you're getting. You don't really know what you're buying or what you're getting and you don't really feel in the mood to . . . shop, let's say, or have the time or whatever. So therefore it seems as if you're at the mercy of some people that you sense, true or not true, have not earned the respect of consumers in the last ten years, let's say. And that's a real thing, you think about it."

Funeral firm chains were mentioned by a few people in the focus groups as a possibility that would minimize this anxiety. With a chain, one could learn of the kind of service provided from family or friends who had used the services of other of the chain's locations. Also, if you moved from one area to another, your experience with an outlet in the previous locale could be applicable to the firm in the new locale.

"But if the funeral director has a chain, I think the family would feel better about it. If he had one out here and one in Chicago, you know it's run by the same type of person. You know what you're gonna get because you have the experience of dealing with him one time, if you liked him or whatever."

5. Half of those surveyed were undecided or had no opinion whether funeral homes should advertise; just under a third thought they should, whereas a fifth thought they should not.

Respondents were asked if they thought funeral homes in general should advertise. One-half of them said they were undecided or had no opinion, and about 20% thought that funeral homes should not advertise. Those who thought that it was desirable for funeral homes to advertise comprised about 30% of all of those surveyed.

94

SHOULD FUNERAL HOMES ADVERTISE?

	%
No, they should not	19.3
Yes, it is desirable	30.4
Undecided or no opinion	50.3

There were no exceptions to or variations in these attitudes by demographic differences. Supplemental Table 40 shows the demographic breakdowns.

The people who were not in favor of funeral homes advertising were asked what the primary reason was that they thought they should not advertise. Most of them felt it was either because it would be in bad taste (41.2%) or because people don't choose funeral homes by the kind of information an ad could contain (37.5%), which was further evidence of preference for more personal sources of information.

PRIMARY REASON FUNERAL HOMES SHOULD NOT ADVERTISE

	%
It would be in bad taste	41.2
People don't choose funeral homes by the kind of information an ad could contain	37.5
Offerings don't vary that much among funeral homes	6.5
It would add to cost	12.6
Other reason	2.1

Respondents were also asked to rank the importance of certain kinds of information to be used in an ad if funeral homes were to advertise. Preferences were quite varied but, in general, information about prices was ranked highest in importance. This was closely followed by the "appearance and 'feel' of the funeral home and staff." Next in the ranking were other characteristics of the funeral home such as religious affiliation, hours, friendliness of staff and personal attention. The types of professional services available, such as coordination of funeral arrangements, driving the limousine, and the location of the funeral home ranked as fourth and fifth, respectively, in importance.

IMPORTANCE OF CERTAIN INFORMATION IN ADVERTISEMENTS FOR FUNERAL HOMES

	Average Ranking
Prices	2.56
Appearance and "feeling" of the funeral home and staff	2.69
Characteristics of the funeral home (religious affiliation, hours, friendliness of staff, personal attention, etc.)	2.92
Types of professional services available (i.e., coordination of funeral arrangements, driving the limousine, etc.)	3.16
Location of the funeral home	3.42

VI. Attitudes Toward Caskets

1. Most people want a casket for themselves, their spouses, and their parents or other family members.

About three-quarters of those surveyed indicated that they would select some kind of casket for themselves, their spouses and parents or other family members. Around 10%, though, said they would not want caskets for themselves or their spouses. About 13% were undecided or had no opinion about caskets. Preference for not having caskets for parents or other family members was 4%.

WHETHER OR NOT TO HAVE A CASKET

	For the Respondent	For the Spouse	For Parents and/or Other Family Members
Would want a casket	73.1	76.6	79.1
Would not want a casket	12.5	10.3	4.0
Undecided or no opinion	14.4	13.1	16.9

Comparison with findings reported earlier shows that this pattern is very similar to the pattern of the preferences expressed for whether or not to have a funeral service.

Geographical location most affected people's preference about whether or not to have a casket. Over one-fifth of those in the West wanted no caskets for themselves, whereas only 7.1% of those in the Midwest wanted no caskets for themselves. Conversely, the West had the lowest percentage wanting some kind of casket for themselves; the Midwest had the highest percentage. In addition, Westerners had the largest percentage of people who were undecided about having a casket.

99

WHETHER OR NOT TO HAVE A CASKET
FOR THE RESPONDENT

	% East	% Midwest	% South	% West
Yes	70.6	79.1	77.5	59.5
No	13.7	7.1	10.3	22.9
Undecided/ no opinion	15.7	13.7	12.1	17.6

In each region, preference for having no casket decreased when applied to one's spouse and it decreased even further in the case of one's other family members. In each instance, Westerners still showed the least interest in caskets and Midwesterners showed the most interest.

% PREFERRING TO HAVE NO CASKET

	% East	% Midwest	% South	% West
For the spouse	11.1	5.6	7.2	21.4
For the parents and/or other family members	3.9	1.7	3.4	8.6

Interestingly, in all regions indecision about caskets for spouses w slightly less than indecision about caskets for themselves. However, ind cision about caskets for parents and other family members was somewh greater than that about caskets for themselves.

100

% UNDECIDED OR HAVING NO OPINION ABOUT WHETHER OF NOT TO HAVE A CASKET

	% East	% Midwest	% South	% West
For the spouse	16.1	11.4	11.3	14.5
For the parents and/ or other family members	18.6	15.5	14.4	20.7

Differences in religiosity, age and experience in arranging funerals had very similar effects on whether or not people wanted caskets. Those who were not very religious were more prone to not want a casket for themselves, their spouses and other family members, than were those who were rather religious.

% PREFERRING TO HAVE NO CASKET

	% Rather Religious	% Not Very Religious
For the respondent	8.6	18.0
For the spouse	6.9	15.0
For the parents and/ or other family members	3.0	5.3

Trends in indecisiveness also paralleled those shown in the regional groups. There was slightly less indecision or lack of opinion about caskets for spouses and somewhat more indecision about caskets for other family. In both instances, those who were not very religious had a greater proportion who were undecided about their preferences for caskets than did those who were rather religious.

101

% UNDECIDED OR HAVING NO OPINION
ABOUT WHETHER OR NOT TO HAVE A CASKET

	% Rather Religious	% Not Very Religious
For the spouse	12.1	14.4
For the parents and/ or other family members	15.2	19.1

The effects of differences in age and experience in arranging funerals are so similar to those of religious differences that they are not reported here, but are shown in Supplemental Tables 41 to 43. Briefly, those who were younger (under 45 years of age) and those who had not arranged a funeral in the last five years had less preference for caskets than did those who were older or had arrangement experience.

Respondents were given a second opportunity in the questionnaire to specify whether they wanted a casket in a question about what kind of casket material they preferred for themselves, their spouses and their other family members. (Their responses to this question are recorded in Supplemental Tables 44 to 46 and are discussed later in this chapter.) Those who chose this "no casket" option provide a basis for comparison with similar results obtained in the 1974 CMA Study. Before making this comparison, however, the current "no casket" responses to the materials question should be examined in light of the "no casket" responses to the casket selection question described earlier.

As shown in the chart below, slightly fewer people chose the "no casket" option in the second question than had done so in the first question. Both the number of people and the percentage of all responses to the question that they comprised are reported.

RESPONDENTS WHO SAID THEY WANTED "NO CASKET"

	For Respondent	For Spouse	For Parents and/or Other Family Members
Question about selecting a casket	N = 177 12.5%	N = 135 10.3%	N = 46 4.0%
Question about selecting casket material	N = 154 10.9%	N = 116 9.1%	N = 41 3.6%

A crosstabulation of these two questions with each other shows that most of those who in the first question wanted "no casket" for themselves or a family member also marked that option for that person in the second question. However, a few of the original "no casket" selectors either did not answer the second question at all or marked "don't know" as their response to it. Only a handful (about 5 people) of those who, in the first question, selected "no casket" for themselves or a family member, indicated in the second question that they would select a wood casket for that person. Thus, the second question appears to be a conservative estimate of the percentage not wanting a casket.

Respondents in the 1974 CMA Study were asked to indicate the type of casket material they would select if they were making funeral arrangements for a member of their family or a close friend. Forty-eight people, which was 4.1% of those who answered that question, said that they would want "no casket." This finding is very similar to the present finding that approximately 4% of the respondents would choose to have "no casket" for their parents and/or other family members. It is questionable, however, whether the 1974 respondents answered that casket material question with their spouses also in mind. If they did, comparison of their answers with the current ones of people who would choose "no casket" for their spouse would suggest some increase in preference for having

103

no casket. However, it is not certain that the 1974 respondents did include consideration of their spouses in their answers.

The present study, therefore, suggests there has not been much change in people's preference for having no casket for parents and other family members. No conclusion can be drawn as to whether there has been an increase in the percentage not wanting a casket for themselves or for their spouses.

2. Most people want a casket that is within their income bracket and that reflects their life style.

Of the people who said that they would want some kind of casket for themselves or other family members, most said that they would prefer one that is within their income bracket. The rest generally wanted a casket below their income bracket. Only eight people out of all those surveyed said they would want a casket for themselves that was above their income level, and only a handful wanted such a casket for their spouses and other family (28 and 29 people, respectively).

KIND OF CASKET PREFERRED
BY THOSE WHO WANTED ONE

	For the Respondent	For the Spouse	For Parents and/or Other Family Members
Casket that is above my income bracket	0.8	2.8	3.1
Casket that is within my income bracket	74.5	82.9	83.1
Casket that is below my income bracket	24.7	14.3	13.1

The pattern of these preferences for kinds of caskets differs from the earlier reported pattern of preferences for kinds of funeral services. Here, the middle range option (the casket within the respondent's income bracket) was generally preferred by about 80% of those surveyed over the less expensive option (the casket below the person's income bracket). However, the middle range option for funeral services (the service typical for the respondent's family and friends) did not receive as large a preference over the less expensive choice (the inexpensive, no frills service). In fact, the majority actually preferred the inexpensive option for themselves, and the typical service was preferred for spouses and other family members by only 52.4% and 59.5%, respectively.

Experience in arranging a funeral within the past five years produced the greatest variations in the findings about casket preferences. Of those who had had such experience, more wanted the middle range casket for themselves than was typical and fewer wanted a casket below their income level. Those without arrangement experience showed less interest in the middle choice and a little more interest in the casket below their wage level.

KIND OF CASKET PREFERRED FOR THE RESPONDENT

	% Who Have Arranged a Funeral	% Who Have Not Arranged a Funeral
Casket above income bracket	1.2	0.6
Casket within income bracket	85.4	69.4
Casket below income bracket	13.4	30.0

Similar variations due to experience occurred in the preferences for casket types for spouses and other family members. These differences were not as large as for the respondent. Since the patterns of preferences for spouses is very similar to that for other family, only the results for the former are shown below. Supplemental Tables 41 to 43 contain the complete information.

105

KIND OF CASKET PREFERRED FOR THE SPOUSE

	% Who Have Arranged a Funeral	% Who Have Not Arranged a Funeral
Casket above income bracket	2.3	2.2
Casket within income bracket	87.3	81.4
Casket below income bracket	10.4	16.4

In addition, males, those who were younger (under 45 years), people with more education (some college or more), and those with higher incomes ($20,000 and over) were less favorable toward the middle range caskets and more favorable toward the lower range ones than were females, those who were older, and those who had less education or lower incomes. The patterns of differences within these four groupings are very similar, so only those for sex are discussed below. The other demographic breakdowns are shown in Supplemental Tables 41 to 43.

More women preferred to have a casket within their income bracket for themselves than men, and fewer wanted a casket below their income level.

KIND OF CASKET PREFERRED FOR THE RESPONDENT

	% Males	% Females
Casket above income bracket	0.8	0.8
Casket within income bracket	69.3	79.6
Casket below income bracket	29.9	19.6

Similar differences existed in preferences for caskets for spouses and for parents or other family members, although to a lesser degree. The breakdown for spouses is shown below.

106

KIND OF CASKET PREFERRED FOR THE SPOUSE

	% Males	% Females
Casket above income bracket	3.0	2.5
Casket within income bracket	81.9	83.9
Casket below income bracket	15.1	13.6

Geographical location also had some impact on preferences for the kind of casket, although to a lesser degree than it did on preferences for whether or not to have a casket or not. Westerners were consistently less favorable toward the middle range casket and more favorable toward a casket below their income brackets than was typical. Midwesterners and Easterners share a greater preference for the middle range and a lesser preference for the lower range casket.

KIND OF CASKET PREFERRED FOR THE RESPONDENT

	% East	% Midwest	% South	% West
Casket above income bracket	0.0	1.2	0.9	0.6
Casket within income bracket	77.7	77.0	72.6	68.8
Casket below income bracket	22.3	21.8	26.5	30.6

There was less variation in preferences for caskets for spouses and other family members. Preferences for parents and other family members are shown below. Supplemental Tables 41 to 43 show the full data.

KIND OF CASKET PREFERRED FOR
PARENTS AND/OR OTHER FAMILY MEMBERS

	% East	% Midwest	% South	% West
One above income bracket	3.3	3.5	3.0	2.6
One within income bracket	82.6	87.9	82.2	81.2
One below income bracket	14.1	8.6	14.8	16.2

Most people in the focus groups felt that the type of casket selected for a funeral was of some importance to other people. Very few felt the casket was not important.

"An awful lot of people take a lot of notice, though, about the casket."

"Well, isn't it an expression of the dignity and esteem you held the deceased in?"

"Aren't those people that are visiting making a judgment upon you as the selector of the thing?"

"I've heard a lot of people say, 'Wasn't that casket gorgeous?' "

"I think people go to the funeral. They don't go tapping on the coffin, you know, to see if it's wood or metal."

People who regarded the selection of a casket to be important did so because they felt that other people would judge them according to the casket they selected. They believed that the quality of the casket would be viewed as a sign of what the selector's true feelings toward the deceased were.

"I think it's because they're so concerned about what other

people are going to think. They don't stop and think about what they can afford and how they feel. They think, 'Oh, well, this is nice but I think I better have that one, because so-and-so might say, "Did you get a load of the crappy thing *she buried her husband in?" And I've heard it at funerals! I was just at a funeral about three weeks ago. It wasn't of an immediate relative of any sort, but I was sitting there and that's all anybody talked about. 'Boy, she really paid a lot of money for that coffin!' You know."*

"My parents talk about, 'My goodness, she sure buried her husband in a lousy way, a lousy casket,' or, 'They sure didn't think much of their mother. Look at that lousy casket!' I didn't realize that, until I had the opportunity and had to do this picking out myself. Then I said, 'Now I know what they're talking about.' "

Many felt that the judgments of others, particularly of relatives, would exert a social pressure strong enough to make them choose a better casket than they would if that pressure were not there.

"But you know the big thing about funerals is when you're kinda pressured into buying a better casket, if not by the funeral director, I don't know, but by your relatives and everybody. And like many people I know, I've never even looked at a casket. I wouldn't know how much that costs. It could be the cheapest one or the most expensive one. I've no idea because I've never looked at them but I've never paid any attention, too, when any of my friends were buried. But I think a lot of people, mostly your relatives too, 'Oh, you can't get a cheap casket, you've got to get a more expensive one!' What's the difference? It's gonna rot away, too."

"No, you know the only reason I would get a steel instead of a cloth-covered wood casket is because I would be pressured into doing it. He's always told me, 'Put me in an orange crate, throw me in the garden,' you know. And he's serious about it! And I can see where a lot of people are taken advantage of when somebody dies. But I think I would be pressured into it, not by the funeral director, but by the relatives. That's why we would definitely like to plan our own funerals."

109

There is a feeling that the funeral director, too, can exert pressure to choose a better casket.

"How can you go to the funeral director that has been dealing with your family for the last six or seven deaths, you know, or a couple of generations? How can you in good faith go with him over to pick out the caskets and he says, 'Well, you know, this is the least expensive.' You know, where they go, 'They're more expensive from here in that aisle,' you know, and they keep going up thousands of dollars. How can you take the least expensive, you have to at least take second best!"

In general, those interviewed felt that the casket a person selects is judged by others to be reflective of that person's own character and worth.

"I've got three children, two in junior high and one in high school. I mean my daughter has just got to have a name on the back end of her jeans or she doesn't want to go to school. Now that to me is keeping up with the Joneses. Some people will do that if they really feel it deep, even into going into funerals. If they will sit there and there's a casket for a thousand dollars, . . . they can afford the thousand, barely, but they can afford that. But the eighteen hundred looks a little better. They'll sit and their thing is, 'Oh, I gotta look good, I gotta look good.' OK, that eighteen hundred dollars, they got to make a loan at the bank to pay for it!"

"My husband told me, 'When I'm dead,' he says, 'don't bury me in the most expensive thing that there is.' I says, 'If you're dead, you're gonna go in the cheapest thing there is.' (Laughter) And his reaction to that was, 'Well, don't bury me in the cheapest thing. I don't want everybody to think that we're real cheap.' Which I probably wouldn't, you know."

There is a consensus that the casket selected should reflect the way the deceased lived — his or her lifestyle. It should be within that income bracket, not below and not over, but what you can afford.

"Well, that depends upon what you can afford. You still have to

110

have a funeral and have something that — you wouldn't just get an old square wooden box and put the body in it ... I would have money for a coffin, not a square pine box!"

"I think it all depends upon your lifestyle. I mean, if you're in the Cadillac and the mahogany box, you've got enough to pay for the whole thing. If you haven't, you just don't look at that."

"In my economic group, no [to a cloth-covered casket]. OK? As a matter of fact, I wouldn't get teak either, even though it's, you know, magnificently beautiful."

People in several groups likened selecting a casket that one can afford to buying a car.

"It was all priced so you know what price. I knew what price range I had to go in and that's where I stayed. It's like going in the car dealer. You pick out what you can afford."

"It's easy to decide if you know what you can afford. It's the same way with a car. If you can't afford a Cadillac, well, then you don't even look at it."

"It is like going in an automobile showroom! Right, 'I like that one but I can afford this one.' "

People feel that those with more money should be able to buy the more expensive caskets. If they had a lot of money, they would do so, too.

"If you have the money, you give the dead as well as the living."

"If they've got the money to buy it, let them buy what they want. You know, it's their choice. You only do it once for the particular person. So if the funds are there ... "

"You're talking about buying the Cadillac. I'd buy the Cadillac. I wouldn't buy that Pinto!"

111

"I'm not saying what other people should do. I'm just saying what I would do. Now if I live in a hundred-thousand dollar house, I'm not gonna have a pine box. That is not my way of living! . . . You do what you can afford."

3. Although people want a casket that is within their income bracket, they also want it to be one at the top of that bracket.

The consensus in the focus groups was that people tend to choose a casket that is the best possible one they can afford, even if it means stretching a little financially.

"You're gonna spend your top dollar, though, I guarantee it. Whatever your budget is, you're gonna spend . . . in your bracket, you're gonna spend at the top of the bracket."

"I happen to be [a widow]. OK? I think like you said, . . . that the Americans want everything, but I think that for a loved person, a person that you got along [with], you want nothing but the best. And this is the last thing you're gonna give to him. I'd been married 37 years. I thought my husband was a wonderful person. He didn't even conduct or tell me what he wanted or anything else, because I done it on my own. But I thought, in my way, since my husband was so good to me, and we wanted nothing but the best for each other, all this time that we worked and everything. All American people want nothing but the best. They don't want to be poverty stricken. They don't want to give their kids anything, they want to give them everything! And I figured, this is the reason that my husband is gonna get everything that I can well afford. I'm not gonna go into the bills that are gonna cost me or that I haven't got the money, but because I thought that I could do it, that's the reason why I did it."

"It's just like, you know, what we were saying, it's just like when you go buy a Chevy or a Cadillac. This is 18 gauge steel or this is bronze, . . . you're buying the importance of the casket. You're putting a loved one to rest, you're gonna do the best you can with the amount of money you've got to spend. So you'll buy the top of the line in your price bracket."

"You know there's one that isn't gonna break you but it's just a little bit. Only another $500."

4. A majority of people feel that what the casket is made of would make no difference to them, and only a quarter feel that it would make at least some difference.

The respondents were asked how much of a difference what the casket is made of would make to them. Over half, 53.1%, said that it would make no difference to them. Another fifth, 21.3%, said it would make only a small difference. Only 25.7% said it would make either some or a lot of difference.

HOW MUCH OF A DIFFERENCE WOULD WHAT THE CASKET IS MADE OF MAKE TO YOU?

	%
It would make a lot of difference to me	8.6
It would make some difference to me	17.1
Total first two categories	**25.7**
It would make only a small difference to me	21.3
It would make no difference to me	53.1

Indifference to casket material was somewhat less among those who said they would select caskets within their income brackets.

HOW MUCH DIFFERENCE CASKET MATERIAL WOULD MAKE TO THOSE WHO WOULD SELECT A CASKET WITHIN THEIR INCOME BRACKET

	For Themselves	For Their Spouses	For Parents and/or Other Family Members
A lot of difference	9.8	8.4	8.4
Some difference	24.2	21.4	21.4
Only a small difference	27.5	26.7	25.5
No difference	38.5	43.6	44.7

Geographical location had the greatest impact on people's perceptions of the significance of what material is used in a casket. People in the West were far more indifferent to casket material, with almost two-thirds of them saying it made no difference to them and only 16.2% saying it made either some or a lot of difference.

HOW MUCH DIFFERENCE
CASKET MATERIAL WOULD MAKE

	% East	% Midwest	% South	% West
A lot of difference	9.7	8.3	11.3	3.3
Some difference	19.4	18.3	16.8	12.9
Only a small difference	19.4	23.2	21.3	20.5
No difference	51.5	50.1	50.6	63.3

Men and women also varied in their perceptions of the significance of the material comprising a casket, with women being somewhat less indifferent than men.

HOW MUCH DIFFERENCE
CASKET MATERIAL WOULD MAKE

	% Male	% Female
A lot of difference	8.8	8.3
Some difference	14.8	19.4
Only a small difference	18.4	24.1
No difference	58.0	48.2

Those people who had less education (high school or less) were also slightly less indifferent to casket material than those with more education (some college or more).

114

HOW MUCH DIFFERENCE
CASKET MATERIAL WOULD MAKE

	% High School Education or Less	% Some College Education or More
A lot of difference	11.4	5.8
Some difference	19.2	15.8
Only a small difference	21.6	20.4
No difference	47.7	58.0

People who were rather religious and had had experience in arranging a funeral in the last five years were also slightly less indifferent to the material comprising a casket. The variations by religiosity and arrangement experience closely resembled those by education, so they are not shown here but are reported along with other breakdowns in Supplemental Table 47.

5. Many people do not know what kind of casket material they would select.

The respondents were asked what kind of casket material they would select for themselves and other family members, given that each material was in their price range. Almost one-third of those who responded said that they did not know what kind of material they would choose.*

THOSE WHO DID NOT KNOW WHAT CASKET
MATERIAL THEY WOULD PROBABLY SELECT

	%
For themselves	30.1
For their spouses	30.2
For their parents and/or other family members	34.2

* *Discussion of those people who did select a certain material follows in the next section. Those who said they would select "no casket" were discussed in a previous section. Supplemental Tables 44 to 46 provide the data from which these results were derived.*

115

This varied somewhat by geographical location. Southerners generally had the highest percentage of people who did not know what casket material they would choose, and Midwesterners had the lowest percentage.

**THOSE WHO DID NOT KNOW WHAT
CASKET MATERIAL THEY WOULD PROBABLY SELECT**

	% East	% Midwest	% South	% West
For themselves	29.0	28.1	33.7	29.0
For their spouses	31.9	26.2	34.7	27.5
For their parents/other family members	34.3	30.1	39.0	33.5

Women, people under 45 years of age, and people who had not had experience in arranging funerals also were more likely not to have a preference for casket material. The breakdowns for age and experience can be found in Supplemental Tables 44 to 46 and are similar to the differences by sex shown below.

**THOSE WHO DID NOT KNOW WHAT
CASKET MATERIAL THEY WOULD
PROBABLY SELECT**

	% Males	% Females
For themselves	25.0	35.2
For their spouses	25.7	35.5
For their parents/other family members	30.8	38.0

6. There has been some increase since 1974 in interest in metal caskets, with well over a third of the people with preferences for certain materials stating a preference for either steel or stainless

116

steel caskets and another fifteen percent wanting precious metal caskets.

Just under two-thirds of those who responded to the question about casket materials indicated a preference for a certain kind of material for themselves, their spouses and their other family members, given that that material was within their price ranges.* Well over a third of these people indicated that they would probably select a steel or stainless steel casket. Over one-third of them stated a preference for a wood casket. Precious metal caskets were preferred by about 15% and fiberglass caskets by around 10%.

WHAT KIND OF CASKET MATERIAL WOULD YOU PROBABLY SELECT?

	For Self	For Spouse	For Parents and/or Other Family Members
Wood	39.0	35.1	33.4
Steel	28.0	28.6	29.7
Stainless steel	9.8	10.9	11.7
Total steel/ stainless steel	37.8	39.5	41.4
Precious metal (e.g., copper or bronze)	12.1	16.3	16.7
Fiberglass	11.0	9.2	8.5

* As noted previously, a majority of the people surveyed in 1981 stated that what the casket is made of would make no difference to them. This is of particular interest, because the question measuring this was asked after the question measuring casket material preferences, thus ensuring that the respondents had already thought about casket material options before reporting how important such casket materials were to them. Therefore, the reported preferences for certain casket materials discussed in this and the following section should be understood by the reader to be general sentiments and not perfect measures of what they would actually purchase.

Comparison of these results with those of the 1974 CMA Study suggests that there has been some increase in preference for metal caskets and a slight decrease in preference for wood caskets. The question asked in 1974 differs in two general ways from the one asked in the current study. First of all, the kind of people for which the 1974 respondents selected casket materials are somewhat different from the kind of people the current respondents were thinking of for their casket material selections. Those surveyed in 1974 were asked to indicate what casket material they would probably select "if you were making funeral arrangements for a member of your family or close friend." The 1974 selections are, therefore, most comparable to the current respondents' selections for their parents and/or other family members. However, since some of the 1974 respondents could possibly have included consideration of caskets for their spouses in their selections of casket materials, the earlier results will also be compared with the current respondents' selections for their spouses.

Secondly, the kinds of casket materials offered as options in the 1974 question were different from the options in the 1981 question. "Wood" caskets were broken down into three categories: "plain wood," "wood covered with cloth," and "polished hardwood." The metal caskets were also categorized differently. Instead of "steel," "stainless steel," and "precious metal" caskets, there were the not quite comparable categories of "inexpensive metal" and "quality metal." In addition, "fiberglass" caskets were listed under the broader category of "fiberglass or other material." A general comparison of the two studies' results is shown in the table on the next page.

The sum of the 1974 respondents' preferences for the three kinds of wood caskets is 39.1%. This is slightly higher than the 33.4% and 35.1% of current respondents who preferred wood caskets for their other family members and their spouses, respectively, and suggests that there has been some decrease in interest in wood caskets.

Comparison of the 1974 and 1981 preferences for metal caskets is best done on the aggregate level. This is because neither of the 1974 metal options is completely comparable to any one of the 1981 options or any combination thereof. "Quality Metal" may have been interpreted by the respondents as referring to "stainless steel" and

118

WHAT KIND OF CASKET MATERIAL WOULD YOU PROBABLY SELECT?

	1974: Member of Family or Close Friend %	1981: Parents/ Other Family Member %	1981: For Spouse %	
Plain wood	9.8			
Wood, covered with cloth	9.0	33.4	35.1	Wood
Polished hardwood	20.3			
Total wood	**39.1**			
Inexpensive metal	15.7	29.7	28.6	Steel
		11.7	10.9	Stainless Steel
Quality metal	32.9	16.7	16.3	Precious metal
Total metal	**48.6**	**58.1**	**55.8**	
Fiberglass and other material	12.3	8.5	9.2	Fiber- glass

even to "steel," as well as to a "precious metal" such as bronze or copper. "Inexpensive metal" could have been thought by some respondents to refer to "stainless steel" as well as to "steel," or even to neither. The aggregate percentage of 48.6% of the 1974 respondents who preferred either inexpensive or quality metal as a casket material is less than the percentages shown for 1981 of those preferring some kind of metal casket. This suggests there has been an increase in preferences for metal caskets.

The preference for fiberglass caskets has not increased since 1974, although it is not clear that it has decreased since part of the larger percentage shown for 1974 may have been attributable to preference for "other materials."

119

7. Most of those preferring caskets within their incomes were more interested in caskets made out of steel, stainless steel, or wood, whereas those preferring lower range caskets were more interested in wood or fiberglass.

Comparison of the casket material preferences reported by those respondents who preferred caskets within their incomes with the material preferences of those wanting caskets below their incomes shows that the different materials were generally regarded as being in different quality categories. The variations between the groups preferring middle-range and lower-range caskets will be discussed first, and then people's preferences for each material will be discussed.

In general, three-quarters of the people who said that they wanted to have caskets within their income level said they would select caskets made out of steel or stainless steel, or else wood. Of the people wanting caskets below their income level, however, three-quarters preferred wood or fiberglass. It should also be noted that precious metal was of interest as a casket material primarily to the group wanting middle-range caskets.*

WHAT KIND OF CASKET MATERIAL WOULD YOU PROBABLY SELECT?

% Wood	% Steel	% Stainless Steel	% Precious Metal	% Fiberglass
For Themselves: Within Income				
30.0	33.6	11.8	16.0	8.5
For Themselves: Below Income				
55.8	18.1	5.0	2.0	19.1
For Spouse: Within Income				
31.1	33.4	11.5	16.8	7.3
For Spouse: Below Income				
55.3	10.7	7.8	1.9	24.3
For Parents/Other Family: Within Income				
28.5	34.0	12.4	18.3	6.8
For Parents/Other Family: Below Income				
48.9	14.8	11.4	3.4	21.6

* *A majority of the handful of people who wanted a casket above their income level also said they would select a casket made out of precious metal.*

120

The preference of those wanting middle range caskets for the metal materials suggests that all of the metal caskets (steel, stainless steel, and precious metal) are regarded as being of higher quality than the fiberglass and at least some kinds of the wood caskets. However, a substantial percentage of the people preferring middle-range caskets wanted wood caskets, which also suggests that some kinds of wood caskets are regarded as being of higher quality. The preference for and meanings of the various materials are discussed further below.

Metal Caskets

People also differed by age and geographical location in their preferences for steel and stainless steel caskets. Although about 38% of both the older and younger age groups wanted to have some kind of steel casket for themselves, the preference for stainless steel over steel varied between these groups. The chart below indicates that more of the people in the less than 45 years group were interested in stainless steel than were those in the older group. As a result, the older group had a higher percentage preferring steel.

WHAT KIND OF CASKET MATERIAL WOULD YOU PROBABLY SELECT FOR YOURSELF?

	% Less than 45 Years	% 45 Years or More
Steel	23.3	31.6
Stainless Steel	14.4	7.3
Total Steel or Stainless Steel	37.7	38.9

These patterns of preferences also appeared in the respondents' choices of casket materials for their spouses and parents or other family members. Supplemental Tables 44 to 46 show the data from which these results were derived.

Geographical differences contributed to differences in the total percentage of people preferring either kind of steel material. Under

121

30% of the people in the East and West wanted either kind of steel casket for themselves, whereas over 50% of those in the South wanted a steel material for their own caskets. The percentages for choice of casket material for spouses and other family members are very similar to those shown below.

WHAT KIND OF CASKET MATERIAL WOULD YOU PROBABLY SELECT FOR YOURSELF?

	% East	% Midwest	% South	% West
Steel	19.1	28.7	36.0	25.8
Stainless steel	9.1	7.3	16.8	3.9
Total steel/stainless steel	**28.2**	**36.0**	**52.8**	**29.7**

People in the focus groups were shown color photographs of caskets made out of different materials.* Responses to the photos showing steel and stainless steel caskets shed further light on the meaning attached to those materials. The steel casket was regarded as looking "about normal," "pretty average," and like a "middle-range" casket. Several people said that they had chosen one like it for a relative for whom they had made funeral arrangements. When shown the stainless steel casket, some people wondered how it differed from the plain steel. Others felt it provided greater durability and that cost more.

"Is there a difference between that and the regular steel?"

"The word 'stainless' automatically makes it more expensive."

"You gotta go to the Mafia to get that one!"

"That won't rust."

* *There were two photographs for each kind of material; one of the exterior of the closed casket and one of the casket with its interior featured.*

122

"Bullet-proof."

"Stainless rusts, not as fast, no. But it does rust."

"It'll take a heck of a long time for it to."

An interesting comment made by one man suggests that the use of the word "metal" to describe a casket, especially when other caskets are described as "steel," may be generally interpreted to mean that the metal casket is made out of "pot metal" and is of poor quality.

"By using the word 'metal' you immediately picture in your mind, when you show steel and metal, you immediately picture in your mind, you got pot metal over there. It's gonna crack when you pick up the handles."

Preferences for caskets made out of precious metals such as bronze and copper varied according to sex, education and geographical location. Women were almost twice as likely as men to prefer a precious metal casket, with about one-fifth of them selecting this option.

PREFERENCE FOR PRECIOUS METAL

	% Male	% Female
For self	8.9	16.1
For spouse	12.8	21.1
For parents/other family members	11.6	23.2

People who had less education (high school or less) also had a greater preference for the precious metals than did those with more education.

PREFERENCE FOR PRECIOUS METAL

	% High School or Less	% Some College or More
For self	17.7	6.5
For spouse	21.0	11.5
For parents/other family members	22.6	11.4

People in the Midwest and the East showed more interest in precious metal caskets than did those in the other two regions.

PREFERENCE FOR PRECIOUS METAL

	% East	% Midwest	% South	% West
For self	12.7	14.6	12.7	5.3
For spouse	17.5	19.4	14.7	10.9
For parents/other family members	21.4	19.1	12.8	11.2

Comments in the focus groups when the participants were shown the photographs of the bronze and copper caskets revealed that a precious metal casket was regarded as a "Cadillac" of caskets.

"It's awful fancy-looking."

"Very impressive."

"It's too expensive."

"That is, I guess, that's the Cadillac of caskets."

People in several of the groups commented on the durability of precious metal.

"Basically, the salesman selling you the casket would say that bronze and copper would be the ageless material, until the advent of the stainless steel and fiberglass. You know. They'd give you the deal that you could go out there with the shovel and fifty years from now you could dig up the thing and reuse it."

"Now the copper one, you could dig that up and reuse it!"

There was a consensus in the focus groups that precious metal caskets were for those who could afford "to put all that money in the ground."

124

"Who should have it? If the family has no regard for money and they have enough. They should have the best. There's no doubt about it."

"If you think it would make you feel good then do it. If there's no remorse for you that you put all that money in the ground."

Wood Caskets

Preferences for wood caskets also varied according to differences in education, experience in arranging funerals and geographical location. Those with more education had a larger percentage preferring wood than did those with less education.

PREFERENCE FOR WOOD

	% High School or Less	% Some College or More
For self	33.2	44.7
For spouse	30.5	39.4
For parents/other family members	27.0	39.1

Those who had not arranged a funeral during the past five years also showed a higher preference for wood.

PREFERENCE FOR WOOD

	% Who Have Arranged a Funeral	% Who Have Not Arranged a Funeral
For self	31.0	43.2
For spouse	31.5	37.4
For parents/other family members	28.6	35.9

125

The fact that the percentages preferring wood for spouses and other family members successively decrease for both of the education experience groups shows that many people are thinking of wood caskets of lower quality. All the findings previously reported indicate that people tend to prefer the caskets for others to be of even better quality than for themselves, and, therefore, the decreasing percentages are probably because those wanting wood caskets for themselves shift to higher quality ones for their loved ones.

Geographical differences for wood caskets split along similar lines as they did for metal caskets. Those in the East and West showed a greater preference for wood caskets than did those in the Midwest, and those in the South showed much less of a preference. Once again, in all of these groups the percentages preferring wood for spouses and parents/other family members successively decrease.

PREFERENCE FOR WOOD

	% East	% Midwest	% South	% West
For self	50.2	40.4	22.8	48.4
For spouse	46.4	36.5	19.7	42.2
For parents/other family members	43.8	33.1	19.2	40.7

Comments from the focus groups on the photographs of a lower-priced cloth-covered wood casket indicated that some people had never seen one and considered it to be "plain," and "cheap."

"Certainly rather plain for what I've seen in all the funeral homes."

"Appears cheap."

"Well, it looks kinda cheap."

"That reminds me of the Depression."

"They maybe use one of these for cremation."

"In my mind I would say it could possibly be . . . It's very plain, nothing wrong with this, it's very respectful. I would say if I just saw the casket closed and there was nothing, you know, and I didn't know who it was, I'd just think there was a minister in it."

The response to photographs of the polished hardwood casket, on the other hand, indicated that material is regarded as fairly expensive, more "traditional," masculine, and high status.

"Now you're getting into some bucks."

"Yeh, I seen one that the guy had that. Beautiful wood there. And that was more expensive, I think, than that steel one."

"I see your hardwood would probably be a more traditional type . . . You know, before they came out with the metal and that, I'd say most of them were hardwood."

"I think that's very masculine looking."

"I would not expect a lady at all."

"I would expect just the connotation of the hardwood and all that to be some big executive."

"Just like the oak panelled executive suite. It just carried right on through to that."

"It's definitely a status."

Several people were bothered by the idea of "wasting" the beauty of the hardwood in a casket.

"My first thought is, that beautiful piece of wood being stuck in the ground! That would drive me crazy! I think I'd come up and haunt someone if they did that. You know, buy a pretty table and think of me when you eat off it, that's what I would think of."

127

"It really should be on a grandfather clock or something."

Fiberglass Caskets

Preferences for fiberglass caskets varied most by geographical location. People in the West and the South showed the most interest in fiberglass.

PREFERENCE FOR FIBERGLASS

	% East	% Midwest	% South	% West
For self	9.0	9.1	11.8	16.6
For spouse	6.4	6.2	11.0	16.3
For parents/other family members	7.9	5.0	10.6	12.7

Some of the people in the focus groups were unfamiliar with fiberglass caskets and said that the one they were shown photographs of was "different" and "modern." Several commented that a fiberglass casket would be lighter in weight. Another comment suggested that fiberglass was perceived as not very substantial and as "lacking something."

"It's gotta be a lot easier on the pall-bearers."

"That wouldn't sell. It's lacking something. What is it lacking?"

A couple of people felt that fiberglass might be more durable than steel or other materials.

"Now that would be better than steel. Probably because it wouldn't rust and steel would rust, if you're worrying about your bones staying together in it."

"It looks like a preservation type thing, where you would put something, you know, to preserve them for the future."

128

However, the general consensus about fiberglass caskets that emerged from the focus group discussions was that they seem "cheap," as the following series of comments, recorded in the order they were made, shows.

"Is that cheaper?"

"Most of it probably is styrofoam covered over with some kind of epoxy."

"Or something similar because it's just molded, you know."

"Yeh, very easy to turn out."

"Let's put it this way. If they have fiberglass, you would, at least I would, I would instantly say, 'Oh, that's gonna be a hell of a lot cheaper.' And if it wasn't I sure as hell wouldn't touch it."

"Right, I would assume too it would be a lot cheaper."

Most felt that they would not select fiberglass, even if it was in their price range, because they felt others would consider them to be cheap if they did.

"I don't know if I would buy a fiberglass one just because it's too new and people might infer that I was cheap if I bought it. I'd rather buy the cheap metal one than the fiberglass even if they're the same price."

8. **The casket attributes considered most important were quality of construction, exterior appearance, protection over the years, and interior appearance.**

Respondents were asked to rank the importance of eight casket attributes. The average rankings for each attribute are shown below, with the attributes ordered according to rank.

IMPORTANCE OF CASKET ATTRIBUTES

	Average Ranking	Difference Between Ranks
Quality of construction	3.43	.08
Exterior appearance	3.51	.39 / .68
Protection over the years	3.90	.21
Interior appearance	4.11	
		.84
Color	4.95	
		.02
Recommendation of the funeral director	4.97	
		.49
Thickness of casket wall	5.46	
		.06
Reputation of casket manufacturer	5.58	

The most important attributes were felt to be the quality of construction and the exterior appearance of the casket. These were ranked, on the average, first and second respectively, and differed by only .08. Protection over the years was ranked, on average, third in importance and interior appearance was generally rated as fourth. The difference between the average ranking of interior appearance and the fifth attrbute, color, is .84. This is larger than the whole range of .68 covered by the first four attributes, and suggests that the first four have a clear precedence in people's minds. Color and the attribute generally ranked sixth, recommendation of the funeral director, were clustered together with almost identical average rankings. The last two attributes differed from them by about .50, and were also very close to each other in average rating. They were clearly of least importance to those surveyed.

These results were very similar to the 1974 CMA Survey findings. "Low price" was added to the 1974 list of attributes, and the specific average rankings are somewhat different from the current rankings. However, the attributes in the 1974 findings have basically the same rank ordering as those in this study.

1974 IMPORTANCE OF CASKET ATTRIBUTES

	Average Ranking
Exterior appearance	3.8
Quality of construction	4.2
Protection over the years	4.2
Interior appearance	4.3
Low price	5.0
Color	5.5
Recommendation of the funeral director	5.7
Thickness of metal or wood	5.7
Reputation of casket manufacturer	6.6

People in the focus groups focused on the appearance or "looks" of the casket in their discussions of what attributes were important. When asked whether appearance or protection was more important, the consensus was that appearance was most important.

"I think we all buy the coffin for its looks. I don't think there is a wooden box — you know, an orange crate would be sufficient."

Most people also favored appearance over other attributes.

"Sometimes, the coffin you might pick out more for eye-appeal than structure, what strikes you for the price."

"I would think that if it was wood and it looked pretty to me it would be just as well as the metal one. Just so it looked nice, or vice-versa, even if it was plastic but it looked nice."

131

Some respondents, however, felt that the quality of construction was the most important attribute, the one necessary to ensure "peace of mind."

"You're definitely buying it because you think you're putting your loved one to rest in a comfortable and a safe and sound structure. I think to sit here and say that we don't care what it's made out of, I think we all do. Maybe not even consciously. This is it, the bottom line, . . . For your peace of mind. And there is a certain amount of that, whether that's an advertising ploy or not, which I think all of us have to a certain degree. If it came to you having to pick out, you know, the arrangements for someone, not yourself, we all talk one way about picking out things for yourself, 'Ah put me in a garbage bag.' But when it comes to doing it for someone else, this is the kind of thing you really are after. You want to know that you did buy a good casket and yet you don't want to feel as if you went overboard."

People placing emphasis on the appearance of the interior of the casket did so with an open casket in mind, feeling that the rest of the casket is not really seen.

"I personally think the inside, the pillow and the mattress makes more of a difference than the type of casket, because, like we said before, the flowers are gonna be covering the casket, so it's important to see this. And in the last funeral homes we've been to I have not seen them open half way. They've always been open the whole way so you really get all that prettiness from the inside. You don't even see the top of it at all unless it's taken out or to the church."

9. **The most important meanings or values that a casket provides are as a symbol of love and concern for the deceased, and as protection to the body of the deceased.**

People were asked to rank the importance of five meanings or values that a casket can provide. The same meanings were used in the 1974 CMA Survey where a measure of how many people found them important was made. The average rankings from the current findings

132

and the measures of importance from the 1974 CMA Study provide similar overall rank orderings of the attributes.

IMPORTANCE OF THE MEANINGS A CASKET PROVIDES

	1981 Average Rankings	1974 % Who Felt It Was Important
Symbol of love and concern for the deceased	2.08	73.6%
Gives protection to the body of the deceased	2.71	66.9%
Expresses personality of the deceased	3.18	49.7%
Provides warmth and beauty during the funeral	3.25	57.9%
Maintains family tradition and pride	3.76	44.0%

The regard for the casket as a symbol of love and concern for the deceased is in line with the focus group findings that people value the kind of casket selected because it reflects to others their true attitudes toward the deceased.

"Well, isn't it an expression of the dignity and esteem you hold the deceased in?"

10. **Half of the public would probably or definitely purchase a casket from some place other than a funeral home if it would save them 20%, whereas only one-fifth would not do so.**

Respondents were asked if they would buy a casket at some place other than a funeral home, if doing so saved 20%. Half of them were favorably inclined toward this idea, with 26.6% saying they would probably do so, and 23.2% saying they would definitely take advantage of the opportunity. Another 28.4% of those questioned were undecided or had no opinion. Less than a quarter, 21.8%, said they were not receptive to such alternative forms of distribution.

WOULD YOU BUY A CASKET FROM SOME PLACE OTHER THAN A FUNERAL HOME IF IT SAVED 20%?

	%
Definitely	23.2
Probably	26.6
Total first two categories	**49.8**
Undecided/no opinion	28.4
Probably not	16.5
Definitely not	5.3
Total last two categories	**21.8**

People in the 1974 CMA Study were asked to state their degree of agreement with the statement, "if it were possible to save 20%, I would prefer to buy a casket from a retail store rather than a funeral home."

1974 PREFERENCES FOR BUYING A CASKET FROM A RETAIL STORE RATHER THAN A FUNERAL HOME IF IT SAVES 20%

	%
Strongly agree	23.7
Agree somewhat	22.3
Total first two categories	**46.0**
Undecided/no opinion	21.2
Disagree somewhat	16.1
Completely disagree	16.8
Total last two categories	**32.9**

134

About the same proportion in this study as in 1974 was receptive to going somewhere other than a funeral home; however, there are now more people who are undecided or have no opinion about the issue. This suggests that there has been a reduction in loyalty to funeral homes as the only outlets for caskets since 1974, although there has not been an equal-sized increase in receptivity to new outlets.

As might be expected, the approximately one-fifth of those respondents who said they would prefer to buy a casket below their income level were more receptive to going some place other than a funeral home to purchase them. Thus, 62.4% of those who wanted the lower range caskets for themselves were willing to go to another outlet.

% OF THOSE PREFERRING CASKETS BELOW THEIR INCOME BRACKETS FOR THEMSELVES WHO WOULD GO TO ANOTHER PLACE TO BUY CASKETS

	%
Definitely	34.8
Probably	27.6
Total first two categories	**62.4**
Undecided/no opinion	22.3
Probably not	12.6
Definitely not	2.7
Total last two categories	**15.3**

As shown below, there was even greater receptivity to alternative outlets among those wanting lower range caskets for their spouses and other family members.

% WHO WOULD GO TO ANOTHER PLACE TO BUY CASKETS

	% Wanting Lower Range Caskets for Spouses	% Wanting Lower Range Caskets for Parents/Other Family Members
Definitely	43.1	48.3
Probably	31.5	27.9
Total first two categories	**74.6**	**76.2**
Undecided/no opinion	15.2	15.6
Probably not	8.2	5.0
Definitely not	2.0	3.2
Total last two categories	**10.2**	**8.2**

Geographical location also affected receptivity to casket distri
butors other than funeral homes. Westerners showed the greate
receptivity, and Midwesterners the least to additional outlets.

% WHO WOULD GO TO ANOTHER PLACE TO BUY CASKETS

	% East	% Midwest	% South	% West
Definitely or probably	46.9	47.0	50.4	57.3
Undecided/no opinion	32.2	25.3	29.8	26.3
Probably or definitely not	20.5	27.6	19.7	16.4

Greater receptivity to alternative outlets was also shown by peop
who were younger, men, those who were more educated, people wi

136

higher incomes, and those who had previously arranged a funeral. Since the results for these groupings were similar to each other, only those for age differences are shown below. The other breakdowns can be found in Supplemental Table 48.

Over 55% of the people under 45 years of age were inclined to go some place besides a funeral home to buy a casket, whereas only about 46% of those older were so inclined. The difference between them was even greater in terms of those who said they were not interested in alternative distribution outlets. (This difference was larger than the ones for the other demographic groupings.)

% WHO WOULD GO TO ANOTHER
PLACE TO BUY CASKETS

	% Under 45 Years	% 45 Years or Older
Definitely or probably	55.8	45.7
Undecided/no opinion	30.5	26.7
Definitely or probably not	13.7	27.6

It should be noted that the 1974 CMA Study found that people who had previously arranged funerals were far less interested in alternative outlets than typical (only slightly more than 10% were reported as agreeing with the idea). This was interpreted to mean that experience enhances appreciation for the professional assistance of the funeral director in decision making. The current results do not replicate that finding and the difference in receptivity between those with experience and those without it is only about ten percentage points — no larger than the difference between the categories in any other grouping.

11. Half of the public are not interested in rental caskets, although 30% are interested and 20% are undecided.

The respondents were asked for their opinions about using a rental casket for display of the body and then using an inexpensive, plain container for placing the body in its final resting place. Over 30% of them said that it sounded awful and that they were totally against it. Another 20% thought that it was all right for others but not for themselves. About 30% said that they either would consider using a rental casket themselves or would actually want to use one. About 20% were undecided on the issue.

OPINIONS ABOUT USING A RENTAL CASKET

	%
Sounds awful and I'm totally against it	30.8
Sounds okay for some but not for me	20.0
Total first two categories	**50.8**
Sounds interesting and I might consider it	21.0
Sounds good and I would want to use a rental casket	8.5
Total preceding two categories	**29.5**
Undecided or no opinion	19.7

People who wanted caskets within their income brackets were less favorable toward rental caskets than was usual. However, those who wanted caskets below their income levels were drastically more favorable toward rental caskets. The breakdowns for respondents preferences for casket types for themselves are shown below. The results for preferences for their spouses and their other family members are similar, although the differences are somewhat smaller.

OPINIONS ABOUT USING A RENTAL CASKET

	% Wanting a Casket Within Their Income Bracket for Themselves	% Wanting a Casket Below Their Income Bracket for Themselves
Totally against it	40.7	16.9
Not for me	25.2	15.7
Total first 2 categories	**65.9**	**32.6**
Might consider it	16.0	37.5
Would want to use	3.3	15.6
Total preceding 2 categories	**18.3**	**53.1**
Undecided/no opinion	14.8	14.3

As these results indicate, the majority of those preferring lower range caskets either would consider or would want to use a rental casket. Although those who prefer caskets below their incomes are only a small segment of the total population (between 15 to 25%), they are an important part of the market for rental caskets.

As might be expected, the same kinds of characteristics that enhanced people's preferences for caskets below their income also enhanced receptivity to rental caskets. Differences in educational level produced the most notable differences. People with some college or more showed more interest in rental caskets. Compared to them, people who had less education had almost twice as many who were totally against the idea of rental caskets and a much lower proportion who were willing to consider using such caskets.

139

OPINIONS ABOUT USING A RENTAL CASKET

	% High School or Less	% Some College or More
Totally against it	41.3	21.8
Not for me	20.2	19.3
Total first 2 categories	**61.5**	**41.1**
Might consider it	14.8	26.6
Would want to use it	6.3	10.6
Total preceding 2 categories	**21.1**	**37.2**
Undecided/no opinion	17.5	21.7

Males, people who were under 45 years of age, and those with incomes of $20,000 or more were also more receptive to rental caskets than females and those who were younger or had lower incomes. Only the breakdowns by sex are below. The others are quite similar and can be found in Supplemental Table 49.

OPINIONS ABOUT USING A RENTAL CASKET

	% Males	% Females
Totally against it	25.7	35.9
Not for me	20.0	20.0
Might consider it	23.5	18.5
Would want to use	11.9	5.0
Undecided/no opinion	18.9	20.6

Westerners showed the most receptivity to rental caskets and Southerners showed the least. Surprisingly, it was not the Midwesterners who were the least receptive to such caskets.

140

OPINIONS ABOUT USING A RENTAL CASKET

	% East	% Midwest	% South	% West
Totally against it	30.1	29.7	37.4	23.3
Not for me	22.4	18.5	19.6	20.0
Might consider it	21.2	24.6	17.0	21.4
Would want to use it	8.1	6.8	7.8	12.5
Undecided/no opinion	18.3	20.4	18.2	22.9

People in several of the focus groups spontaneously mentioned rental caskets as being a desirable way to provide a high-quality, expensive casket for a loved one and meet the expectations that relatives or friends have about the kind of casket that should be used.

"The ideal funeral set-up would be to rent the bronze and be buried in [a middle-range casket]."

"Maybe you could just rent one and switch 'em or get something else later."

"Nobody and none of your relatives would know about it."

Several, however, felt a rental casket would not be appropriate if there was to be a graveside ceremony.

"What about us people who stand there and watch the body go down into the grave? You know, you can't switch it then if you're watching while you're putting the body in the grave. We make it a point to stay there."

Some did not like the idea of a rental casket because they did not like the idea of moving the body from it to its final container.

"I wouldn't want the body moved all the time . . . No, I'd just leave it. I think the body's had enough. Just leave it in there and let it go. If I picked out one too expensive, I'd get another."

141

VII. Attitudes Toward Disposition of the Body

1. Most people still prefer burial in the ground as the means for putting the deceased to rest, but there has been an increase in the proportion of people preferring cremation.

Respondents were asked what means of putting the body to rest they would arrange for themselves, their spouses, and immediate family members or close friends, if the decision were up to them. Over 58% said they would choose burial in the ground for themselves, 20% said they would prefer cremation, about 10% preferred to donate their bodies to science, and 4.2% wanted to be entombed above ground. The preference for burial increased with arrangements for spouses and other family members and friends. Interest in cremation and donation to science decreased somewhat. About 7% were undecided or had no opinion about what they would arrange for themselves and their spouses, and 12.3% didn't know about what they would decide for their other family or friends.

PREFERRED ARRANGEMENTS

	For Self	For Spouse	For Immediate Family Member or Close Friend
Burial in the ground	58.6	64.9	69.4
Cremation	20.2	17.8	11.2
Donation to science	9.8	4.8	3.1
Entombment above ground	4.2	4.8	3.6
Burial at sea	0.6	0.5	0.2
Other	0.5	0.2	0.2
Undecided/no opinion	6.0	6.9	12.3

The people surveyed for the 1974 CMA Study were asked a similar question: "If it were entirely up to you, how would you like to have your body disposed of after you have died?" Fewer options were given them than in the current study: "burial," "cremation," donation to a medical school or science," and "indifferent." Their responses are shown below along with the current respondents' preferences for themselves. For the purposes of comparison, the 1981

145

options of "burial in the ground," "entombment above ground," "burial at sea," and "other" have been recategorized as "burial," and "undecided/no opinion" has been recategorized as "indifferent."

PREFERRED ARRANGEMENTS FOR SELF

	1974 %	1981 %
Burial	63.0	63.9
Cremation	14.2	20.2
Donation to medical school or science	13.4	9.8
Indifferent	9.4	6.0

These results indicate that people's preferences for arrangements for themselves have not changed a great deal since 1974, although a slight increase in interest in cremation and decrease in interest in donation to science and in indifference is suggested.

The 1974 respondents were also asked, "If you were making funeral arrangements for someone in your immediate family or a close friend who had no funeral instructions, what would you probably arrange?" This question varies from what the 1981 respondents were asked in two ways. First, the 1981 respondents were asked to respond separately for their spouse and for their immediate family members/close friends. The 1974 question does not specifically mention spouses so it is not certain whether those respondents took spouses into consideration in their answers. Secondly, the 1981 question did not qualify that the arrangements to be chosen be for those "who had left no funeral instructions" as did the 1974 question. Therefore, the current respondents probably took into account any known preferences of the people being considered, whereas the 1974 respondents probably did not. In spite of these differences, comparing the results of the two studies still provides an indication of attitude change. The 1974 answers and the 1981 answers for spouses and other relatives and friends are shown together below, with the 1981 results again recategorized.

146

PREFERRED ARRANGEMENTS FOR OTHERS

	1974 %: Immediate Family or Close Friend	1981 %: Spouse	1981 %: Immediate Family or Close Friend
Burial	82.1	70.4	73.4
Cremation	7.8	17.8	11.2
Donation to medical school or science	3.1	4.8	3.1
Indifferent	7.0	6.9	12.3

These results suggest that there has been a decrease in interest in burial since 1974 and some increase in interest in cremation. The 17.8% who were interested in cremation is of note because it is a segment of the population who consider cremation not just for themselves but also for others.

Differences in geographical location, education and religiosity affected people's preferences for arrangements most, with differences in income level and experience in arranging funerals having some impact also. The following discussion of the effect of these demographic differences will focus only on people's preferences for "burial in the ground" versus "cremation" because selection of the other options did not vary noticeably by demographic differences. The demographic breakdowns for all the options are shown in Supplemental Tables 50 to 52.

People in the West, as might be expected from the large percentage of them interested in no funeral service or casket, had the highest percentage of people interested in cremation, with over one-third of them selecting that option for themselves. They also had the lowest percentage selecting burial in the ground for themselves. Midwesterners and Southerners, on the other hand, showed the greatest interest in burial in the ground, with over two-thirds selecting this for themselves. They also had the least interest in cremation.

147

PREFERRED ARRANGEMENTS FOR THEMSELVES

	% East	% Midwest	% South	% West
Burial in the ground	59.1	64.5	64.1	41.0
Cremation	20.9	14.4	15.7	34.9

Regional differences in selections for spouses had the same pattern. All but the Westerners showed an increase in preference for burial over cremation.

PREFERRED ARRANGEMENTS FOR SPOUSES

	% East	% Midwest	% South	% West
Burial in the ground	63.6	73.5	71.9	43.1
Cremation	17.6	11.4	12.8	35.4

Preferences for burial over cremation were even greater when people were asked to consider what they would arrange for someone in their immediate family or a close friend. About a quarter of the Westerners, however, still preferred cremation.

PREFERRED ARRANGEMENTS FOR
IMMEDIATE FAMILY MEMBERS OR CLOSE FRIENDS

	% East	% Midwest	% South	% West
Burial in the ground	67.9	76.7	76.7	49.2
Cremation	12.8	5.3	7.9	23.3

People who had attended some college or more also had more

interest in cremation than those with less education. Almost a quarter preferred it for themselves, and over a fifth wanted it for their spouses. And people with higher education were twice as likely as those with less education to want cremation for their spouses and immediate family members or close friends.

PREFERRED ARRANGEMENTS

		% High School or Less	% Some College or More
For self:	Burial	70.0	48.6
	Cremation	13.8	26.3
For spouse	Burial	73.0	57.4
	Cremation	12.1	23.1
For immediate family/close friend:	Burial	74.3	64.7
	Cremation	7.6	14.4

Respondents who were not very religious also had a greater preference for cremation than did those who were rather or very religious. Over a quarter of them preferred cremation for themselves and their spouses.

PREFERRED ARRANGEMENTS

		% Rather Religious	% Not Very Religious
For self:	Burial	66.1	48.3
	Cremation	13.3	29.9
For spouse:	Burial	71.3	56.2
	Cremation	12.5	25.1
For immediate family/close friend:	Burial	75.7	61.2
	Cremation	6.6	17.1

People with higher incomes ($20,000 or more) and who had no arranged funerals in the last five years also had more interest in cremation than did those with lower incomes and who had arranged funerals, although the percentage of each group wanting cremation was less than those described above. The breakdowns of the differences by income and arrangement experience can be found in Supplemental Tables 50 to 52.

The focus group interviews provided insight into why people have positive or negative attitudes about burial and cremation. Some people's comments showed that their choice of burial or cremation was strongly determined by the image in their minds of how the body of the deceased would look in its final resting place and form. For example, one man related his preference for burial over cremation to the comfort he derives from the mental picture he has of his mother in the ground, looking much as she did in life. He objected to cremation because it would change the body's "configuration."

"Unless the body is deformed by accident or sickness or something, you know, if you view the body, I'd keep it. Like my mother, she wasn't deformed in any way and she wasn't sick that long before she died. So she looked almost the same laying in the casket as she did in life, except color and things like that. And I have that picture of her. And I picture her in the ground as that. And I like that. To think that she's . . . I think that [cremation is] a terrible thing to do to a human being."

This man's later comments suggest that the desire to be able to think of the deceased in the ground as looking much like the person did in life is directly related to a preference for a casket that offers a high degree of protection.

"And with those vaults and everything else, you won't get your leakage or anything else, I'm told. It doesn't wash away and so forth. There is a place to go visit. There are lead vaults and people have been exhumed many, many years later in contemporary time. And the body is the same as it was at the viewing."

The desire to have a pleasant mental image of the body of the deceased person also can create a preference for cremation if the body is deformed by accident or sickness.

150

"The only experience I had with cremation is just the last two funerals I was at. It was my cousin and his wife — they were burned to death. At the time it was closed coffin. His parents just felt, you know, well they wouldn't have a cemetery plot and put out an extra two thousand dollars for a plot, so when they're, when you can't recognize them any more anyway. It was quick, one of those situations that they just felt, . . . well, we'll cremate them and get it over with."

Cremation in such a situation may help "cleanse" the image of the deformed body from the survivors' minds and lets their mental picture of the deceased be one of what the person looked like when alive and well.

The tendency to picture the body in its final resting form and place affected preferences for burial versus cremation in another way, too. Many people said they did not want to be buried or cremated because of the bodily sensations burial or cremation would entail. In other words, their sense of how burial or cremation would "feel" and what the body would "experience" affected their preference for one of those means of disposition.

Before illustrating this, it must be mentioned that some people did claim not to care at all what happened to their bodies after death.

"Do it whichever way you want . . . Because when I'm dead you're not gonna know it."

"When I die and my body stops functioning, I really don't care what happens at that point . . . When I'm dead, I told my wife, get a big baggie! . . . When I'm dead, I'm dead!"

"When you're gone, you're gone. It really doesn't make that much difference, you know."

However, others noted that although rationally they believed that what happened to their bodies after death should not matter, the concept of cremation still bothered them.

"I, you know, assume that we have a soul and that this is an instrument that we use during life and once you die, you know,

151

the soul leaves the body and this is just a piece of material. You know. Really. Assuming that, I would say that there should be no reason for not going with cremation. However (laughs), your body would be..."

"*We all say it doesn't make a difference. Why are we worried about a casket that preserves the body? But I think, ah, and yet at the same token I'm as guilty, at least I'm just thinking my own thoughts, and yet I'm not so sure that I could be an organ donor or donate my body to medical science. So if I really don't care what happens to the body, then how come I'm not willing to donate my body to medical science or how come I get a little squeamish when I think about cremation? . . . Whereas a lot of people, cremation wouldn't bother them at all.*"

Of those who were sensitive to what the body would feel, most indicated that they did not want to be "burnt up." Some others felt that it would be "cold" to be buried in the ground or put in a crypt.

"*It depends on whether you want to be in the ground or in a drawer. I always thought going in a drawer was cold. I really thought it was worse than being buried. Every time you look into a crypt at the cemetery it just, I don't know, it's just creepy or something.*"

"*But, you know, I think it's terrible cold, too, on a winter day, when I think they're down there in that ground and it's cold. See, that bothers me.*"

"*But have you ever looked into a crypt on a cold winter day? It's colder in there!*"

There was also some repugnance expressed about the idea of worms getting to the body if it was buried in the ground. This makes people desire either another means of disposition or a casket or vault with a high degree of protection.

"*I don't feel like being stuck up in a casket . . . and you know that old song, 'The worms crawl in and the worms crawl out'? Yeh. That's what it's gonna be. You're just gonna be a skeleton.*"

"That's what my husband's aunt says. She doesn't want the worms."

"That's the reason my grandmother wanted to be cremated. She didn't want worms crawling through her body."

(Husband) "She just wants to be cremated because she doesn't like to go in the ground. Because there are worms down there and she doesn't like worms."

(Wife) "I hate them!"

The focus group discussions also revealed other reasons for preferences about burial and cremation. Most people favored burial because it is traditional, "the way it has always been done," and the appropriate means for showing respect for the person.

"I think it's just that everybody does what the family does. You know, you go by tradition. And if there ain't been that many people cremated in the family, it's outrageous to even think of it. 'I'll be darned if I'll do that!' "

"I think it's burying your body, it's putting the person to rest. You just don't throw them away, you have to do something and you have to do it in a nice way."

"Well, because we've always done it!"

"If he went before me I'd bury him. My father always said that he wanted to be cremated and we went and bought a cemetery plot! He's gonna be buried, I don't care what he says. Because to me it just seems like, well I think I'd be going against God by just burning up his body . . . it's the fact that the body's buried in the ground and to me that's the way it should be."

Along the same lines, some people preferred burial because it provides a memorial of the deceased person that the survivors can visit and take comfort from.

"And if you did want to go, say if you had nothing to do on a Sunday and you just happened to be there, maybe you'd say,

153

'Let's go and just see what the grave looks like or the headstone, or whatever.' "

"There's still a tie there. Something material on this earth."

Such people were very disturbed by cremation (which seemed by definition to mean scattering the ashes) because it provides no material reminder of the deceased's existence and survivors have no place to visit.

"I wouldn't want to be cremated. I don't know exactly why, because I'm not gonna know what happens anyway."

"I would like underground. That doesn't bother me for some reason. But cremation, I wouldn't. I would like to think that my children and grandchildren would have a place to come and see. Like, I get great solace when I go back home to Maryland and I can, right after church, go out and see my mother's grave."

"I just don't relish being placed in a damn furnace and being burnt up so there's nothing. I have a friend that I was in the service with, it was [John Doe] and he was cremated. I loved the guy, and I think there is no [John Doe], there's some ashes somewhere. He had them scattered someplace. There's no grave, there's no body . . . it's all burnt up and gone. I have no place to go."

Cremation was worrisome to a few people because it seemed to them to be very final and irrevocable.

"If you get cremated and they develop a way to bring us back to life, you're gonna be a sad product!"

Those who favored cremation had a variety of reasons for doing so. Most of the people in the California focus group said that they preferred cremation because it made things easier for survivors. It minimizes grief and simplifies arrangements.

"It's like people are always trying to do what they think is right. And now people seem to be saying that they want to do

154

something that feels good and not always stick with tradition."

"This is what my husband keeps telling me. He says, 'Well,' he says, 'if I go before you, I want to be cremated.' He says . . . 'You don't have to go through all that hardship and every-thing.' He says, 'I'm gone, so what? You still keep on living.' "

"That's what [cremation with scattered ashes] I prefer. It's simple. I don't think there's any 'why' to it. Death is essential-ly an irrational matter anyway. It seems like a reasonable and efficient way to take care of it . . . The grief of the people that are living is far minimized."

A few people in the other focus groups also favored cremation for the same reasons.

"What my husband's wishes are. He says, 'When I die, I don't want you to take me to a funeral parlor and have this big lavish thing.' He says, 'You take me and have done whatever has to be done to prepare my body. Have me cremated and have the funeral right away. Get it all over with.' He says, 'If you can do it all in one day, fine. And then, have people come to the home and have it over with, where you're not lingering. You've lingered long enough in your own mind even after the funeral.' He just thinks it's very barbaric to have people come and sit there and stare at you. And everybody cries and everybody's this, and your turmoil inside is tremendous at that point."

"My husband always says, his reasoning for thinking of the cremation is to get it over with. A funeral should be a happy time. You should be happy for the individual because they are finally at total peace at that point. The instant that you're gone, your soul leaves, why mourn it? You should be happy that the person has finally gotten out of all the trouble and tribulations, that they're finally with the Lord now. [The traditional funer-al] irritates the daylights out of him."

Several people in the California group felt that cremation was easier on survivors because, since the ashes were scattered, there was no need to visit and maintain a graveside or to feel guilty if one failed to do so.

"Myself, I just want to be thrown away. I'm in charge of the cemetery. I have brothers and sisters but I'm the one who's convenient. It depresses me to go there. I take care of the grave site. I don't want somebody to have to do that for me. I really want to be just blown away. That brings up a thought. My parents died quite a few years ago now. Actually, I don't remember. I think it was my older sister and my husband, who naturally wouldn't be as emotionally involved, who took care of the arrangements. My sister chose (the cemetery) because it was kind of between where both of us lived. But I feel guilty at times, usually I don't, but there are times when I feel . . . I should really be going decorating for Mother's Day when we go to the grave. And I really didn't get anything out of it. I remember one time I was gonna arrange to meet my sister there, but she says she can't stand to go there. So just my husband and I went there and her daughter came and met us. But she apparently can't stand to go there, just doesn't want to go there. I don't get anything out of going there. The few times we did go there I didn't like it. It's depressing. And I think, although I didn't think I would be that way at the time, that God apparently, or whatever you believe in, nature, God, the way we're made, you do get over deaths almost amazingly. At the time you don't think you will. As time went by, as I say, I can talk about my parents' death. I don't know, it seems strange in a way that it doesn't bother me, because I was very close, yet if it weren't that way, everybody'd go crazy. It has to be that way. But the fact that having the graves you shouldn't be visiting, doesn't really fit in with whatever nature or God's way, of having us get over these events that have taken place in our lives. So in a way it would be better (to have) the cremation idea."

"I . . . want to be cremated because I can remember when my husband was killed and he was buried in one of the veterans cemeteries. And every time, even to this day, I could drive by there and you always feel this horrible guilt that you don't go there and visit. And all it is is just cut stone. And I just don't want anybody to ever feel guilty that they're not visiting a stone and not thinking about me. I'd rather have them think about me as the way I was."

156

"As far as we're concerned, me and my wife, we're thinking of cremation, we call ourselves thinking about our children. Maybe we're not. Maybe they, my son's thoroughly opposed to it. But I see what my wife goes through when she leaves to go to the cemetery for flowers at Christmas and on their birthdays and stuff like this. And she was an only child. And it thoroughly, it just tears her up. And I wouldn't want to put my children through this."

It should be noted that a few people in the other focus groups favored cremation because of the same idea mentioned in connection with burial — wanting to be able to remember the deceased as he or she was when alive. They did not want their mental image of the deceased to be one of a dead person.

" . . . I don't like going there, either, to sit and stare at the casket and stare at the body. I want to remember him when he was alive."

"In the discussions that I've had with my wife, number one, I don't like to remember anybody dead, I like to remember them alive."

Some interest in cremation also stemmed from the fact that its lower cost was thought to make it more practical. The money that would be spent on burial could then be used in other and better ways.

"I'm leaning toward it [cremation] because of the economics for one thing. I have a feeling my kid could do more with that money if I left them a few thousand dollars."

"Well, they just did a show on TV about it. You can get yourself cremated for about $250. Why pay $3500, have everybody in there sobbing and getting hysterical? Just go get cremated and that's the end. You can take the money and have a party."

"I'd rather have my children take the money and go to Hawaii. Every time I see a cemetery, I think of what a beautiful park it would have been for children to play in."

"For one thing, I think my husband would be disappointed if I, he's always been so very practical. I don't think he'd be very happy if I went all out like that. On the other hand, . . . it's traditional in my family, on my side. In certain respects, some of my nicest memories were the festivities, it seemed like a real special occasion. But, in my own mind, I just don't feel that I could share my feelings or this emotion with people popping out from ten years back or so. I don't even know if I'd, ah, . . . 'cause sometimes I would be suspicious of their motives. So I would go the practical way [cremation], and I think my husband would like that, because he's even more so than I am."

The focus group interviews also provided insight into people's respons to donating their bodies to science. Generally, people feel that it is commendable and even practical thing to do, in theory.

"I see some value to medical science . . . Everybody in this room does not think of themselves dying. Truthfully! . . . But, I mean, I could sit here right now and I could be gone, you know. So nobody is planning on it. Some people do it. Of course I don't plan on dying. But I have to admire people that do, because science does need this, somebody's got to do it."

"I heard that a lady we knew, that was a neighbor of my mother's, passed away last week. And we were quite surprised because when the daughter called my mother she says that, 'My mother had donated her body to science. There will be no wake or no funeral and the body will be cremated afterwards.' They were Catholic and we were kind of surprised that that happened. But it's an alternative! My mother was thinking about it and I seen her after that and she says, 'Well, you know, she might have something. Look at the expense she saved!' . . . You know, that's an alternative that's worthy of our thought."

As a personal matter, however, they are not interested in donating th own bodies to science. They are not as opposed to simply donati organs.

"You can be put in little jars, one here and one there . . . That sounds more, I mean if I had a diseased organ, they could take that and check. But what do they need with my fingers and my toes and ears?"

"Well, there's a difference between donating your body for science and donating organs. There's a big difference."

"What about medical school where students dissect the body and then study?"

"That's different from donating organs."

"There's two separate things here."

"Yes, but if you've donated your body to science and they're gonna dissect . . ., do an autopsy and mess around with the parts, no, no, no!"

"No, I don't like."

One of the reasons people are put off by the idea of donating their bodies to science is that the body's configuration, its completeness and integrity, would be destroyed.

"That's frightening though, when I think of somebody poking around in my dead body."

"Or making fun of it, you know. Like, 'Look at that dead stiff!' Who needs that?"

"I don't want them to chop me up."

"You can be put in little jars, one here and one there . . ."

People were also quite bothered by the painful sensations and further deterioration to which they thought the body would probably be subjected.

"They use your body to inject you with certain deadly chemicals and see how they react and they give you serum."

"Oh, no! Your body still lives for quite a while! Your hair grows in the grave! Your body lives . . . I mean, when I say living, your body functions for 'X' amount of time."

159

"My husband had eight by-passes by the time he died. Eight! Can you imagine giving his body now, after he's been cut up already eight times, and he suffered all that time, and now he's gonna donate the good part of his body for research? . . . Yes, it would be valuable for everybody else. But he was suffering . . . so much . . ."

A few people felt that if a person was to be cremated anyway, it would be more acceptable to donate the body in total or to donate organs.

"If he's gonna be cremated, I think that's definitely what I would do. You know, give the eyes and everything. I think it would be super."

Dismembering a body that will be reduced to ashes by cremation is not objectionable because one's mental "picture" of the cremated person is not like his "configuration" in life anyway. It is, however, highly distasteful if the body is to be buried, because the mental picture it creates of the body in the grave is grotesque, unnatural, and disquieting.

2. **Almost half of those who favored cremation wanted the ashes to be scattered, with a fifth wanting burial and another fifth undecided.**

Respondents who had indicated that they would probably arrange cremation for themselves, their spouses, or other family or friends were asked what they would like done with the ashes. Around one-half of them wanted the ashes scattered and somewhat under one-fifth said they wanted them buried in the ground. Another fifth were undecided and about 10% preferred they be entombed above ground, such as in a columbarium. Under 10% said they wanted the ashes to be retained in the home.

WHAT WOULD YOU LIKE DONE WITH THE ASHES?

	Of Self	Of Spouse	Of an Immediate Family Member/ Close Friend
Scattered on land or sea	50.3	49.0	44.7
Burial in the ground	16.1	17.2	20.3
Entombment above ground (i.e., in a columbarium	7.2	8.2	12.0
Retained in home	5.1	8.1	3.5
Undecided/no opinion	21.2	17.5	19.5

VIII. Attitudes Toward Pricing

1. The average estimate of the price of a funeral, not including a cemetery lot or vault, is $2400.

Respondents were asked for their estimates of the average price for a funeral, including the casket, facilities and service, but not the cemetery lot or vault. The average estimate for all respondents was $2400, and over twenty-five percent felt a funeral would cost $3000 or more.* The distribution of the estimates is shown below.

ESTIMATES OF THE AVERAGE PRICE FOR A FUNERAL

	%
Under $1000	3.6
$1000-1499	10.9
$1500-1999	17.6
$2000-2499	23.4
$2500-2999	14.7
$3000-3999	17.9
$4000 + over	11.9
Total $3000 + over	**29.8**

Age and geographical location affected people's estimates of the price of a funeral most. People under the age of 45 estimated that a funeral would cost them about $2470, whereas those who were 45 years or older thought it would be about $2320, or about $150 less. People in the West gave the lowest estimate, about $2050, whereas those in the Midwest thought the price would be about $2600, or almost $550 more.

ESTIMATES OF THE AVERAGE PRICE FOR A FUNERAL

	Estimate
West	$2049
South	$2513
Midwest	$2597
East	$2314

* The average price estimated in the 1974 CMA Study was $1450. The effects of inflation render the price estimates in the two studies incomparable.

Differences in income, sex and experience in arranging funerals also had some effect on funeral price estimates. Those with higher incomes, males, and those who had arranged a funeral in the past five years had somewhat higher average estimates of the price of a funeral than did the rest of the respondents.

ESTIMATES OF THE AVERAGE PRICE FOR A FUNERAL

		Estimate	Difference
Income	$8000 to $19,999	$2307	$171
	$20,000 or more	$2478	
Sex	Male	$2462	$119
	Female	$2343	
Funeral Arrangement Experience	Have arranged	$2480	$105
	Have not arranged	$2375	

2. People feel, on average, that a funeral should cost $1500, or about $900 less than what they think it really does cost.

The respondents were also asked to indicate what they thought the average price for a funeral *should* be. The average that people said a funeral should cost was $1500. This is about $900 less than the $2400 average of their estimates of what it actually costs. The distributions of the preferred funeral prices are shown below. Almost a quarter said they thought the price of a funeral should be under $1000, and only 10% thought it should be over $3000.

WHAT THE PRICE FOR A FUNERAL SHOULD BE

	%
Under $1000	24.3
$1000-1499	28.0
$1500-1999	16.2
$2000-2499	16.0
$2500-2999	5.6
$3000-3999	6.6
$4000 + over	3.4
Total $3000 + over	**10.0**

People's estimates differed considerably according to several demographic factors. Chief among these was geographical location, with those in the West stating a preferred price that was over $350 lower than the average one, and Midwesterners indicating a preferred price that was over $125 higher than the average of the total estimates.

WHAT THE PRICE FOR A FUNERAL SHOULD BE

	Preferred Price
West	$1138
South	$1567
Midwest	$1628
East	$1547

Experience in arranging funerals also had a strong impact on what people were willing to pay for funerals. Those who had arranged a funeral in the past five years on average thought that a funeral should cost about $1735, which was $235 more than the average of all the estimates. People without arrangement experience, on average, said a funeral should cost about $1400, which was $100 less than the average.

167

Religiosity, level of education, and age also affected people's perceptions of preferred prices for funerals. Larger than average prices were tolerated by those who were rather religious, who had less education and those who were 45 years or more in age. Those who were less religious, less educated or younger preferred lower than average prices. Income also had some effect on preferences, with people earning less than $20,000 a year having a lower than average preferred funeral price and those earning $20,000 or more wanting close to the average preferred funeral price of $1500.

WHAT THE PRICE FOR A FUNERAL SHOULD BE

		Preferred Price	Difference
Experience Arranging Funerals	Have arranged	$1737	$332
	Have not arranged	$1405	
Religiosity	Rather religious	$1600	$247
	Not very religious	$1353	
Education	High school or less	$1589	$184
	Some college or more	$1405	
Age	Less than 45 years	$1434	$116
	45 years or more	$1550	
Income	Less than $20,000	$1438	$97
	$20,000 or more	$1535	

Participants in the focus group interviews generally considered funeral prices to be high. A few felt that these prices were justified, mostly because of the high cost of maintaining the funeral facilities and staff and the probability that every funeral home must have periods when no funerals are scheduled at it.

"Funeral directors, you know, it isn't like they've got a morning, noon and night funeral every day of the week. So they've got expenses and if they only get three funerals a week . . . so they've got a lot of expenses which is one of the reasons I think why the prices are high."

A few felt that they got their money's worth even in light of high prices because funeral homes and directors offer needed services at a difficult time so that they don't have to personally worry about such things.

"Yes, when you think about it, when you walk into the funeral home, . . . I mean, let's face it, you have got a rotting body on your hands. Somebody comes, the paramedics or the ambulance comes, they take 'em away and you, thank God, there's somebody to help drain that blood out of there and put that stuff in there and take care of it. That I am very grateful for, . . . because that's something we all don't want to do. The law says that we have to bury our dead, we can't just go out and throw them in the, . . . you know. So all these things and then, just think, you come there and you walk in and it's there, your loved one is there, sort of straightened up. Everything is done for you. So, you know, it's just like buying a meal. Some people don't mind paying money for food — others, it kills them. But I really think it's worth it, because when I have to do that, I don't want to have to worry about anything about it. I just want to go and get it over with and I really, I think they're worth it."

There is some feeling that although funeral costs are too high, funerals represent an expense that happens only rarely in a lifetime.

"Let's put it this way. The average person, he's getting stung once or twice in his life. So that's why you really don't care. Unless you've got a huge family and live to be 120."

"He's got a good point there. I thought about it a long time ago. I mean what's all this talk about this and that. You get hit one time and you're through. When I left the undertaker, when everything was all over, I got the insurance money, it took about 30 days, and I went over and I paid him. And that was

it. The show was over as far as I was concerned. That's the last bill I'll pick up out of my own pocket.

Some people felt that they did not really know whether or not they were getting their money's worth from funeral costs because they had no factual basis upon which to make a judgment. One usually does not shop around and any one area has only a few funeral establishments. Also people don't generally discuss funeral prices, except amongst close family, because it is a very personal matter, just like one's income.

"I perceive [a funeral costing] $3500 to $4000. How do we know that you couldn't get the best, the same funeral for $2500? There's no concept of whether 5000 bucks is good or bad. Now wait now! Really! . . . If you live in Palatine, there's only two or three funeral homes in Palatine. You live in Schaumburg, there's only two or three. OK. I mean, you're in an area, you don't want to go all the way to Glenview, if you don't have anything to do with Glenview, to save 500 bucks."

"I would say most of the time, it's not a topic of conversation, that comes up. 'How much did you pay for it?' You know, it's like asking somebody how much they make. That kind of conversation just doesn't come up. Or maybe within the family or something . . . Nobody's ever asked me about that kind of thing."

This feeling of not knowing the true costs of funerary services was related to the feeling that funeral directors have power over their customers and are in a good position to take advantage of them. (See Chapter V).

Many of the focus group comments shed some light on why people generally wanted funeral prices to be lower than what they were. Several participants said that they felt that it was too bad to have to spend a lot of money on a funeral because what was received in return was only a momentary experience. The same money could have purchased something of more lasting value.

"But you don't enjoy it that much. I mean, you know, with a car you're gonna enjoy it for a few years. And that's over and

done with and you don't see anything for it. I think that's what a lot of us feel. It's an awful lot of money and you don't, how many days can you sit there and look at the person in the coffin? You have to get it over with."

The high costs of funerary services are felt to put too heavy a load on people. If corners have to be cut to survive financially, then it is better to economize in areas that do not affect everyday affairs, like funerals.

"Really, I know I'm a cheapskate at heart, I know this. But I'll spend money on something that needs, where the money needs to be spent. You know. For instance, if I want a freezer, I buy the best freezer. I don't want a cheapie. But when you really think of it, it is just a pure waste of money. We all, every single one of us has to die. It should be a part of our natural thing . . . But the thing is, I think there should be some kind of a movement on to get the cost down, to really as minimum as possible. Really, especially in these days of inflation. You know a lot of people are just barely making it."

Attitudes toward the profits made by the funeral industry also contributed toward people's interest in lower funeral prices, as will be discussed in the next section.

3. **On average, people think that 48% of the price of a funeral is profit for the funeral home and that this profit should be only about 26%.**

Respondents were then asked to estimate what percentage of the price for a funeral is profit for the funeral home after all costs and expenses are deducted. The average of these estimates was 48%, which was somewhat higher than the estimate in the 1974 CMA Study of 42%.* The distribution of the current estimates is shown below. Over a quarter felt that funeral firms make a 60% or larger profit.

---

* *The 1974 average percent profit estimated may be slightly lower, as the indexed average is unavailable and the males had a slightly lower average estimate than females (40% versus 43%).*

WHAT PERCENTAGE OF THE FUNERAL PRICE IS PROFIT?

	% Respondents
Less than 10%	0.9
10-19%	5.5
20-29%	14.9
30-39%	10.6
40-49%	11.8
50-59%	28.5
60-74%	9.8
75-100%	18.1
Total 60% or more	**27.9**

The estimates did not vary by demographic characteristics or funeral arrangement experience.

Respondents were then requested to specify what they thought the percentage of profit *should* be. The average of the amounts indicated was about 26%, which was about 22% less than the amount of profit generally thought to be built into funeral prices. Over a quarter, in fact, felt the profit should be under 20%.

WHAT SHOULD BE THE PERCENTAGE OF PROFIT?

	% Respondents
Less than 10%	3.6
10-19%	24.3
20-29%	41.6
30-39%	10.9
40-49%	7.3
50-59%	10.2
60-74%	0.7
75-100%	1.4

Only Westerners varied noticeably from this pattern, in that more of them, one-third, felt that the percentage of profit should be under 20%.

The consensus in the focus groups was that the profit earned by funeral firms is sizeable.

"You want to talk mark-up or profit? Even the profit I'm sure is phenomenal. You know that most of these places are supporting many families, you can have three or four generations in the business. They're affording them enough money to live that way. I think they're entitled to it. Everybody else is making money."

"The mark-up in a funeral home is like the jewelry business, it runs on, I'd say, close to a 60% mark-up. The only thing that sets him off is that he has to pay for all that grounds, the parking space and the lot. But after he gets over that, it's all free. On the average — it's $4000 to bury them, right? Now, if I was an established funeral director, I could take that $4000 and I bet you could skim close to $2000 off of that, it seems to me."

"Well, very bluntly, there's two businesses you'll never see folding up. That's McDonald's and funeral homes . . . It's undoubtedly profitable . . . Why? because . . ., like I said, there's so many of them and none of them are out of business."

"Funeral directors make a lot of money."

"I don't know any poor ones."

"What the hell, they use their equipment and premises over and over, you know. All that's depreciatory you know. The funeral home is a write-down as far as the business is concerned. The cars are a write-down with tax. So he works it all out. Probably a conservative 50%. It's a wild, wild business!"

As the following dialogue shows, however, some people felt that a large profit was warranted, because this profit must carry firms through periods when they have no work.

173

"A 30% profit on any given funeral wouldn't be that bad because he may have five funerals this week and two next week. And he might have ten the next week."

"And nothing the week after that."

"Right, and he can be sitting there looking out the window for a week, too."

Others felt that the high profits they perceived funeral directors to earn were justified by the demands the work places on them and the benefits of the personal attention that they can provide.

"His hours are basically long. Quite long."

"He can be called at 2:00 in the morning or whenever it happens."

"Get over to the hospital to pick up the body or anything else. Also the other services of him going to the hospital, picking up the body. He has to pay his staff. He could have a good week and a very bad week. It's not a continual basis. And I think you don't mind paying for the funeral as long as he took care of you. You can go to some funeral parlors, they kind of give you that non-personal business feeling. But you can go to some other funeral homes, maybe, that's why I picked this one out. He knew the family and everything else. He talked with you as a counselor more so than just a businessman, though you knew that he had the Cadillac parked in the back and everything else."

Some people did express uneasiness with the perceived high profits. Some felt, as shown in the following dialogue, that although the job is demanding, it is something the funeral director chooses to pursue. He does not carry as many burdens as other high profit professions.

"My doctor makes more dough than they do because he has more business."

"He's taking more responsibility, too. He's taking more respon-

174

sibility, a doctor is, than the funeral director. Basically, you know, he prepares the body and puts it in the coffin which the customer has purchased.

"It's not a pleasant job."

"Well, it's like nothing else, you know. He's chosen to do this."

"So you're paying for it."

Still others were uncomfortable with the perceived high profits of funeral directors because they felt that most people work just as hard for a living but do not get such high returns.

"If the guy is half-way honest, I don't think, — if he makes 50%, you know, I think he's entitled to this. He's doing you a service. The biggest item was the casket."

"He's doing you a service? We all work for a living, but do we make 50% of — you know?"

4. People believe, on average, that about 41% of the funeral price is for the casket, about 35% is for the professional services and around 24% is to cover the cost of the facilities.

Respondents were also asked to estimate what percentage of a funeral's price is used to cover the costs of the casket, professional services (coordination of arrangements, etc.), and facilities (buildings, furnishings, etc.). The average of the estimates of the percentage covering casket costs was 40.8%. The portion thought to cover services was, on average, 34.7% and that for facilities was 24.5%. These percentages were similar to those in the 1974 CMA Study, where the average estimates for the casket, services and facilities were 40.5%, 29.9% and 21.7%, respectively. However, the 1974 average percentages add up to only 91.1%. Because the 1974 averages do not account for the whole funeral price, the discrepancies between the two studies' percentages for the casket, services and facilities cannot be interpreted as showing attitude changes over time. At most, a comparison of the two sets of findings suggests that people still perceive the casket to be the most expensive element in a funeral.

When the 1981 respondents were asked to indicate what they thought the percentages for the casket, services and facilities *should* be, they answered with essentially the same percentages as above.

WHAT PERCENTAGE OF THE FUNERAL PRICE COVERS EACH OF THE COMPONENTS?

	Estimate of Actual %	What the % Should Be
For the casket	40.8	42.3
For the services	34.7	32.8
For the facilities	24.5	24.9

People seemed to feel satisfied with how they believe the funeral price is distributed over the three main elements of a funeral.

5. Most people believe that funeral prices are rising about the same as the cost of medical and hospital care and the overall cost of living.

When asked whether they thought funeral prices, compared to medical and hospital prices, were rising faster, about the same, or slower, around two-thirds of the respondents said they thought funeral prices were rising about the same. Around 23% said they were rising slower, and 14% said faster. These results are very similar to the 1974 CMA Study findings.

COMPARED TO MEDICAL AND HOSPITAL CARE, FUNERAL PRICES ARE:

	1981 %	1974 %
Rising faster	13.6	11.3
Rising about the same	63.6	62.4
Rising slower	22.8	26.3

176

The only change in this pattern occurred for people who had previously arranged a funeral. Only about half of them thought funeral prices were rising about the same as medical and hospital prices, and 30% of them thought funeral prices were rising slower. Among people who had not arranged a funeral within the last five years, a few more than average (68%) thought funeral prices were rising about the same as medical prices.

COMPARED TO MEDICAL AND HOSPITAL CARE, FUNERAL PRICES ARE:

	% Who Have Arranged a Funeral	% Who Have Not Arranged a Funeral
Rising faster	16.8	12.3
Rising about the same	53.6	67.9
Rising slower	29.6	19.8

The respondents were also asked to compare the rise in funeral prices to the rise in overall cost of living. Again about two-thirds said that they thought both were rising about the same. However a few more (21%) thought that funeral prices were rising faster than thought they were rising slower (13%). This is a slight change from the 1974 answers which had roughly the same number feeling the rise was faster as felt it was slower.

COMPARED TO THE OVERALL COST OF LIVING, FUNERAL PRICES ARE:

	1981 %	1974 %
Rising faster	20.9	16.0
Rising about the same	66.5	66.9
Rising slower	12.6	17.1

177

Basically, people perceive the rate of increase in funeral prices as being comparable to that in medical prices and the overall cost of living, as in 1974.

6. Most people prefer itemized pricing, although a third prefer unit pricing.

As in the 1974 study, the current respondents were asked to state their preferences for one of three pricing methods: unit pricing where one price is given which includes all costs; functional pricing where three prices are given, one for the casket, one for the facilities and one for the professional services; and itemized pricing, where prices are given for specific services and facilities and for the casket. About 50% of the respondents said they preferred itemized pricing. Just over one-third said they wanted unit pricing and only about 16% wanted functional pricing. These percentages are very similar to the 1974 CMA findings.

PRICING METHOD PREFERRED

	1981 %	1974 %
Unit pricing	34.0	34.3
Functional pricing	16.5	16.7
Itemized pricing	49.6	49.0

People who were 45 years or older, those with less education, and those with incomes between $8000 and $19,000 were slightly more favorable than average toward unit pricing, and those who were younger, had more education or had higher incomes were slightly more favorable than average toward itemized pricing. Breakdowns for these characteristics are shown in the following table and further breakdowns are shown in Supplemental Table 53.

178

PRICING METHODS PREFERRED

		Unit	Func-tional	Item-ized
Age	Under 45 years	26.8	17.4	55.8
	45 years or over	39.6	15.4	45.0
Education	High school or less	39.4	15.4	45.1
	Some college or more	29.2	17.5	53.4
Income	$8,000 to $19,999	36.7	15.2	48.1
	$20,000 or more	27.7	18.2	54.1

Although a few of the participants in the focus groups said they liked unit pricing, many other people had negative things to say about it. Most of these comments indicated that they felt unit pricing was used by funeral directors to get the customers to pay for extras they may not want or use.

"In our particular case, my mother-in-law's wishes were that the facilities at the undertaker's were not used at all, which we paid for, . . . it was a package deal which we paid for. All that was done at the undertaker's was that the body was prepared and we had graveside services and that's all there was . . ."

"I think it's wrong but these were her wishes and because he said this was 'a package deal, if you don't use it, that's your hard luck.' And again I didn't dicker with him on that fact. But we didn't use any of the facilities . . . there was no written prices anywhere, he just quoted package prices. He never showed us a price list. There was nothing."

"Years ago it used to be that they set it up, and you paid for the coffin separately, you paid for your limousine separately, and all this other stuff. Now, this package deal, there is things that you might not even use in this package that you don't even know about. And that's what he tells you. He'll say, 'How

179

many mourners is there?' and you'll say, 'Well, I have my own car.' 'Well, we can cut the car out.' But you might have paid for that car for all you know. You never know! A funeral director is a gentleman's gentleman. You can't ask for a softer, nice-spoken guy that . . . (laughter). But he's in business for the money."

Many in the focus groups said they preferred itemized pricing because it would enable them to avoid having to pay for extras while letting them understand each of the costs involved.

"I like the itemized package too. I mean having it all itemized out instead of saying, 'Hey, this casket is $5000 and that includes all the services.' Then they show you another one for $3000 and that includes all."

"This funeral home on the south side. They were very, very efficient. They laid out a sheet of paper, there were all the dollar figures there. You could go up or down on any particular item. They did not have a package deal, at least they didn't propose one. You kind of build your own package . . . I think 90% of the time when you build your own package you're gonna do better than when they give you a package . . . It was all itemized straight on down. There were a lot of little nittie-gritties, fineties that I said, 'That's just so much extra money,' and . . . I was able to delete those."

"In fact, if I had to go someplace else . . . Having been through it, the next place I think I would have them itemize everything, if I didn't trust them — or not 'trust' — didn't understand it."

7. **Around half the people would not be interested in an extended payment plan for a funeral, although about one-fifth would be interested and 30% are indifferent or don't know.**

When asked whether they would use an extended payment plan if it were available at the funeral home, 51% of the respondents said they either would probably not use it (25.5%) or would be almost certain not to use it (25.6%). Another 30% said they were indifferent or didn't know, and only 19% indicated they probably would or

180

almost certainly would want to use an extended payment plan. These results vary somewhat from the 1974 findings in that there has been a large increase in the number of indifferent or undecided people and some decrease in both the number who are interested, and the number who are not interested in such a plan.

ATTITUDES TOWARD AN EXTENDED PAYMENT PLAN

	1981 %	1974 %
Would be almost certain to use	5.0	5.0
Would probably use	14.1	21.4
Total first two categories	**19.1**	**26.4**
Indifferent or don't know	29.8	16.4
Would probably not use	25.5	34.4
Would be almost certain not to use	25.6	22.9
Total last two categories	**51.1**	**57.3**

The current results varied somewhat according to differences in age and experience in arranging funerals. Almost a third of those who were 45 years or older said they would be almost certain not to use an extended payment plan, whereas only half as many of the younger people (15.4%) felt that way. The older respondents were also less prone to be undecided than were the younger ones.

ATTITUDES TOWARD AN EXTENDED PAYMENT PLAN

	Those Under 45 Years	Those 45 Years or More
Would be almost certain to use	7.9	3.1
Would probably use	15.7	12.9
Total first two categories	**23.6**	**16.0**
Indifferent or don't know	37.6	24.3
Would probably not use	23.4	26.9
Would be almost certain not to use	15.4	32.5
Total last two categories	**38.8**	**59.4**

181

More of those who had arranged a funeral in the past five years also were certain that they would not use an extended payment plan than were those without arrangement experience. Fewer of those with experience indicated that they probably or certainly would use such a plan than did those who had not arranged a funeral.

ATTITUDES TOWARD AN EXTENDED PAYMENT PLAN

	Those Who Have Arranged a Funeral	Those Who Have Not Arranged a Funeral
Would be almost certain to use	5.2	4.9
Would probably use	10.8	15.4
Total first two categories	**16.0**	**20.3**
Indifferent or don't know	25.6	31.6
Would probably not use	26.1	25.2
Would be almost certain not to use	32.3	22.7
Total last two categories	**58.4**	**47.9**

Further demographic breakdowns can be found in Supplemental Table 54.

IX. Market
Segmentation

1. There are two segments in the funerary market: those who desire "no frills" services and those who prefer more "typical" services.

Up to this point, the focus of this report has been on the description of individual questions in the survey and their interpretation. The data can also be analyzed by looking at many questions at once and by seeking how people's answers are related. On the basis of such an analysis, the people surveyed can then be classified into separate groups. These groups are market segments, each of which is a group of consumers who share common attitudes, in this case, for certain kinds of funerary services.

Segmentation analysis was performed using the statistical technique of cluster analysis. Cluster analysis is a multivariate technique which enables a researcher to analyze responses to a number of survey questions all at once, and then classify people into groups on the basis of this analysis. The cluster analysis done for this chapter used people's answers to seven questions.*

The seven questions used were primarily financial in nature. These questions are taken as defining the consumer's basic propensity to consume funeral services. Two of the questions measured the respondents' desires for a certain kind of funeral service. They were: (1) "What kind of funeral service would you prefer for yourself?" and (2) "For a funeral of this kind, what would you expect it would cost?" The first question provides a verbal measure of funeral types, and the second gives the respondents' financial interpretations of each type. Similar questions were used to measure preferences for casket prices: (3) "What price of casket would you select for each of the following?" and (4) "For a casket of this kind, what would you expect it would cost you?" Also, two questions were asked about the over-all average prices of funerals: (5) "What would you estimate to be the average price paid for a funeral?" and (6) "What do you think this price should be?" Finally, an equity measure was used to reflect what would be fair to spend: (7) "What do you think the percentage of profit (for the funeral firm) should be?"

---

* *Use of more questions (variables) was prohibited by the capacity limit of the computer cluster program used.*

185

A random sample of 300 of all survey respondents was used for the cluster analysis.* Examination of the distributions of answers to each survey question in both the sample and the original group revealed that the sample was representative of the larger group.

The cluster analysis uncovered two basic consumer segments. These segments were then analyzed to see how they differed from each other in terms of answers to all the other questions in the survey. The largest segment, comprising 196 people or about two thirds of the sample, can be referred to as the No Frills segment. The other segment, consisting of the other third (102 people),† can be called the Typical Services segment. The segments differ from each other because their members prefer different kinds of funeral and casket offerings.

Broad characterizations of each market segment are made in the next two sections on the basis of all the survey questions. Obviously for any one question there are some members of each segment that do not have the same preferences as their cohorts. The focus here is on overall patterns of difference. The tables at the end of this chapter show the breakdowns for each segment's answers to key questions.

It should be noted initially that the segments do not differ strongly on demographic characteristics. For example, the two segments do not differ from each other in terms of the sex, age or education of their members.

2. The No Frills Segment, comprising about two-thirds of all those surveyed, is interested in putting less money, energy, and time

* *The use of a sample and its size of 300 was necessitated because of the capacity limits of the cluster program used. The sample consisted of 150 men and 150 women who were randomly selected from the 381 men and 740 women comprising the survey respondents.*

† *The number of people in the two segments sum only to 298, not 300, because 2 of the respondents in the sample were so different from the others in their answers that they were not included in either of the basic segments.*

into funeral experiences, not because they are more casual about funerals but because they have definite preferences for certain funeral practices and want to control their funeral experiences and are defensive in their contacts with the funeral industry.

Funeral Experiences

Although a majority of the No Frills Segment members have had the usual kinds of experiences in attending and arranging funerals, compared to the Typical Services Segment about a third of them participated in only a limited fashion in the funeral they most recently attended. They were less likely to attend the wake, visitation or calling hours for the person whose funeral it was, and/or they did not go to the cemetery service. For another third, the funeral itself was less involved. For example, fewer (less than a dozen) flower arrangements were at the funeral.

The fifth of the segment who had personally arranged a funeral in the past five years were careful to control the context within which they arranged the funeral. They were accompanied to the funeral home by one to four people and were either the primary decision maker or participated equally with others in the decision making.

Funeral Homes and Services

No Frills people place less of an emphasis on having a preferred funeral home. About half have their "own" funeral home and the other half do not.

Most say they would want to have some kind of funeral service for themselves, their spouses and/or other family members, but about a fifth say they would want no funeral service at all for themselves. Those who do want a service opt for the inexpensive, no frills kind, and estimate it will cost less than $2000.

Ten minutes is perceived by most No Frills members as being the longest that speakers' comments at a funeral should take. They want the wake to last only one or two days. Although most feel the casket, if present, should be open at some point in the funeral period, a fifth want no casket present at all.

187

Disposition of the Body

Most segment members favor putting the body of the deceased to rest by burial in the ground. However, this segment also consists of those in the general population who prefer cremation, and over a quarter of the No Frills Segment would want themselves and their spouses to be cremated.

Caskets

The subgroup within the No Frills Segment which favors cremation is evidenced by the quarter of the segment who prefer to have no casket for themselves and the fifth who prefer no casket for their spouses. The majority of the segment members, however, do want caskets for themselves and family members, and want them to be caskets within their income brackets. However, about one-third want caskets below their income brackets. People wanting caskets estimate they would cost less than $1100 each.

Most feel that what material a casket is made of would make no difference to them. And, although a little over a half of the segment members are positive toward the use of rental caskets, almost as many are against it.

Preplanning

No Frills members are not casual toward the funeral experience, and are receptive to preplanning. A full half of them and their spouses have already made their wishes known about their funeral preferences to their families. However a majority are unaware of preneed arrangements being available to them from a funeral firm in their locale.

Pricing

People in this segment estimate that the average price for a funeral is less than $2400, but feel that it should be less than $1500, a discrepancy of at least $900. A defensive stance toward the funeral industry is suggested in this, and in the fact that they prefer itemized pricing. The majority would not want to use an extended payment plan or are indifferent or don't know.

Demographics

No Frills members tend to have incomes of $20,000 or more, and are as likely to be not very religious as to be fairly religious. They are more likely to live in the East and West, as would be expected due to population distribution patterns.

3. The Typical Services Segment, comprising a minority of only one-third of the funerary market, wants to keep funeral experiences traditional because they want to do what is correct, and are willing to depend on funeral personnel to help them do so.

Funeral Experience

People in the Typical Services Segment are more likely to participate in most aspects of the funerals they attend, by going to the wake or visitation, and the cemetery services. Over a third of them have arranged one or more funerals, and went to the funeral home with two to four other people. They did not have as prominent a role in the decision making as did those in the No Frills Segment, however, and usually participated equally with others in the decision making.

Funeral Homes and Services

Members of this segment have preferred funeral homes, and virtually all of them want a funeral service to be held for themselves and their family members. The kind of service they prefer is that which is typical of their family and friends. They estimate such a service would cost $2000 or more.

They prefer to experience all aspects of a funeral to the fullest and want the speakers' comments to be at least fifteen or more minutes in duration. They want the casket to be open at least at some point during the funeral period and want the wake or visitation period to last at least two to three days.

Disposition of the Body

People in the Typical Services Segment want themselves and their family members to be buried in the ground.

Caskets

Members of this segment want everyone in their families, themselves included, to have a casket, and in particular, one that is within their income brackets. They estimate that such a casket would cost well over $1100, and what the casket material is would make a difference to them. They are quite positive toward the idea and use of rental caskets.

Preplanning

This segment is casual about preplanning, and most of them and their family members do not discuss their wishes with each other. This is true even though most of them have heard of local funeral homes offering preplanning arrangements.

Pricing

Those in the typical services segment estimate that the average price for a funeral is over $2400, although they think the price should be $1500 or more. They prefer that unit pricing be used, although many also are open to the itemized pricing method, and are generally opposed or indifferent to using an extended payment plan.

Demographics

The members of this segment are evenly divided between lower and upper income brackets, live mostly in the Midwest and South and are fairly religious.

190

Tables showing detailed breakdowns of differences between the No Frills and Typical Services Segments.

FUNERAL EXPERIENCE

		No Frills Segment	Typical Segment
Number of funerals attended in past five years	None	16.0	5.8
	1 or more	84.0	94.2
Number of wakes etc. attended in past five years	None	23.9	10.6
	1 or more	76.1	89.4
Attendance at wake at funeral most recently attended	Yes	62.0	85.1
	No	38.0	14.9
Number of flower arrangements present at funeral most recently attended	More than 12	65.4	77.4
	1-12	30.8	22.6
	None	3.8	0.0
Was the casket open at funeral most recently attended?	Yes	83.3	91.1
	No	16.7	8.9
Attendance at a cemetery service at funeral most recently attended	Yes	65.8	81.1
	No	34.2	18.9
Number of funerals arranged in the past five years	None	78.0	62.9
	1 or more	22.0	37.1
Role in making funeral arrangements	Primary decision maker	37.1	28.5
	Participated equally with others	39.4	54.3
	Participated but others had more important role	18.5	14.3
	Participated by carrying out preexisting detailed plans	5.0	3.0
Number of people accompanying participant to funeral home	0	9.5	6.0
	1	28.6	17.1
	2-4	42.8	62.7
	5 or more	19.1	14.2

191

FUNERAL HOMES

		No Frills Segment	Typical Segment
Do you have a preferred funeral home?	Yes	52.8	73.5
	No	47.2	26.5
How would you rate that funeral home?	Excellent	61.7	54.7
	Good	35.3	44.0
	Fair	3.0	13.

FUNERAL SERVICES

		No Frills Segment	Typical Segment
Would you want a funeral service to be held for you?	Yes	80.0	100.0
	No	20.0	0.0
Would you want a funeral service for your spouse?	Yes	84.6	98.8
	No	15.4	1.2
Would you want funeral services for your parents and/or other famliy?	Yes	90.4	100.0
	No	9.6	0.0
What kind of funeral service would you want for yourself?	Stands out	0.8	1.0
	Typical	25.0	63.9
	No frills	74.2	35.1
What kind of funeral service would you want for your spouse?	Stands out	2.0	2.4
	Typical	35.6	71.8
	No frills	47.0	25.8
What kind of services would you want for your parents and/or other family?	Stands out	3.5	1.3
	Typical	50.4	78.9
	No frills	46.0	19.7
What do you think it would cost for the kind of funeral service you would want for yourself?	Less than $2000	77.9	2.0
	$2000 or more	22.1	98.0
What do you think it would cost for the kind of funeral service you would want for your spouse?	Less than $2000	62.9	11.8
	$2000 or more	37.1	88.2
What do you think it would cost for the kind of services you would want for your parents and/or other family?	Less than $2000	46.6	1.1
	$2000 or more	53.4	98.9
How much time should be devoted to the speaker's comments at a funeral service?	Only 5 to 10 minutes	59.1	45.8
	15 or more minutes	40.9	54.2
Do you prefer the casket open, closed, or not present during the funeral?	Open	60.7	84.6
	Closed	19.1	14.3
	Not present	20.2	1.1
How many days should the wake/ visitation period take?	1 day	44.7	24.5
	2 or more days	55.3	75.5

192

DISPOSITION OF THE BODY

		No Frills Segment	Typical Segment
If it were up to you, what would you choose for yourself?	Burial in the ground	55.4	77.6
	Cremation	31.1	7.1
	Other	13.5	15.3
What would you choose for your spouse?	Burial in the ground	66.5	80.2
	Cremation	24.8	5.5
	Other	8.7	14.3
What would you choose for your parents and/or other family?	Burial in the ground	78.3	85.7
	Cremation	15.4	6.0
	Other	6.3	8.3

CASKETS

		No Frills Segment	Typical Segment
Would you want to have a casket for yourself?	No	23.8	0.0
	Yes	76.2	100.0
Would you want to have a casket for your spouse?	No	17.9	1.1
	Yes	82.1	98.9
Would you want to have a casket for your parents and/or other family?	No	7.9	1.2
	Yes	92.1	98.8
What kind of casket would you prefer to have for yourself?	One above my income bracket	0.0	0.0
	One within	63.4	82.5
	One below	36.6	17.5
What kind of casket would you want your spouse to have?	One above	0.0	4.7
	One within	80.9	86.0
	One below	19.1	9.3
What kind of casket would you want your parents and/or other family members to have?	One above	0.9	1.2
	One within	82.0	87.8
	One below	17.1	11.0
What do you think it would cost for the kind of casket you would want for yourself?	Less than $1100	79.0	26.3
	$1100 or more	21.0	73.7
What do you think it would cost for the kind of casket you would want for your spouse?	Less than $1100	68.9	32.6
	$1100 or more	31.1	67.4
What do you think it would cost for the kind of casket you would want for you parents/other family?	Less than $1100	87.1	47.3
	$1100 or more	12.9	52.7
How much difference would what the casket is made of make to you?	At least some difference	38.7	66.9
	No difference	61.3	33.1
What do you think about rental caskets?	Positive response	55.3	85.2
	Negative response	44.7	14.8

PREPLANNING

		No Frills Segment	Typical Segment
Have you made your wishes known to your family about what kind of funeral you want?	Yes	51.3	38.6
	No	48.7	61.4
Has your spouse made his or her wishes known?	Yes	50.0	36.6
	No	50.0	63.4
Have your parents and/or other family members made their wishes known?	Yes	41.1	46.3
	No	58.9	53.7
Are you aware of preneed arrangements being offered by a funeral home in your area?	Yes	44.3	56.0
	No	55.7	44.0

PRICING

		No Frills Segment	Typical Segment
What would you estimate is the average price paid for a funeral?	Less than $2400	63.3	31.4
	$2400 or more	36.7	68.6
What do you think this price should be?	Less than $1500	61.2	17.6
	$1500 or more	38.8	82.4
Difference between the estimated average price for a funeral and the price it should be	Less than $950	38.8	23.5
	$950 or more	61.2	76.5
What do you think is the average profit for the funeral firm?	Less than 48%	29.6	38.2
	48% or more	70.4	61.8
What do you think the profit should be?	Less than 26%	51.0	53.0
	26% or more	49.0	47.0
What kind of pricing method would you prefer for funeral prices?	Unit	28.9	44.0
	Functional	16.0	18.0
	Itemized	55.1	38.0
Compared to medical and hospital costs, how are funeral costs rising?	Faster	10.2	11.8
	The same	64.8	61.8
	Slower	25.0	26.5
Compared to the overall cost of living, how are funeral costs rising?	Faster	19.4	23.5
	The same	68.9	63.7
	Slower	11.7	12.7
Would you use an extended payment plan?	Yes	16.8	21.6
	Indifferent or don't know	32.6	31.4
	No	50.6	47.0

194

DEMOGRAPHICS

		No Frills Segment	Typical Segment
Family income	$8000 to $19,999	42.2	50.0
	$20,000 and over	57.8	50.0
Region	East	26.0	18.6
	Midwest	26.0	35.3
	South	25.5	34.3
	West	22.4	11.8
Religiosity	Fairly religious	50.3	69.6
	Not very religious	49.7	30.4

X. Appendix: The Questionnaire

SECTION 1

The following questions deal with attendance at funerals. We realize this may be a difficult topic, but it is one of importance to everyone at certain points in life.

1. How many funeral services have you attended in the PAST FIVE YEARS for family members, friends and acquaintances? (Please check the appropriate box in the FIRST column below.)

   How many times have you attended visitation/calling hours or wakes in the past 5 years? (Please check the appropriate box in the SECOND column below.)

	Number of Funerals Attended	Number of Visitations/Calling Hours/Wakes
0	☐ . . .	☐
1-4	☐ . . .	☐
5-9	☐ . . .	☐
10-14.	☐ . . .	☐
15-19.	☐ . . .	☐
20 or more.	☐ . . .	☐

If you indicated that you have attended NO FUNERALS, please skip to Section 2.

2. How many funeral services have you attended in the past 5 years for each of the following? (On each line in column 1 below, please write the number of funerals you have attended for the category of people. If you have attended no funerals for a category of people, please write "0" on that line.)

3. In the second column below, please write an "X" in the appropriate box to show which ONE of the funerals you attended MOST RECENTLY. (If you have attended only one funeral, please "X" that one as most recent.)

	Number Attended	Most Recently Attended (Please "X" only 1 box)
Spouse	☐ . . .	☐
Mother	☐ . . .	☐
Father	☐ . . .	☐
Son or daughter.	☐ . . .	☐
Brother or sister.	☐ . . .	☐
Grandparent.	☐ . . .	☐
Other relative	☐ . . .	☐
Close personal friend	☐ . . .	☐
Acquaintance or other person.	☐ . . .	☐

Please answer the following questions based on the particular funeral that you indicated in Question 3 was the one you most recently attended. Just check ONE box for each question.

4. Did you go to the funeral home before the funeral service, that is, during the visitation/calling hours or the wake?

Yes . . . . ☐   No, there were no visitation/calling hours/wake . . . . ☐

No, although there visitation/calling hours/wake . . . . ☐   Don't recall . . . . ☐

5. Where was the funeral service held?

Funeral home . . . . ☐   Other. . . . . ☐

Church or synagogue . . . . ☐   Don't recall . . . . ☐

Cemetery. . . . . ☐

6. How many people attended the funeral service?

Less than 10. . . . . ☐   80 or more. . . . . ☐

Between 10 and 39 . . . . ☐   Don't recall . . . . ☐

Between 40 and 79 . . . . ☐

7. Were limousines used to transport the family and/or close friends of the deceased?

Yes, there were 2 or more limousines . . . . ☐   No . . . . ☐

Don't recall . . . . ☐

Yes, there was 1 limousine. . . . ☐

8. Were flowers present at the funeral service?

Yes, more than a dozen flower arrangements . . . . ☐   No . . . . ☐

Don't recall . . . . ☐

Yes, several (4-11) arrangements ☐

Yes, but only 1, 2 or 3 arrangements . . . . ☐

9. During any part of the funeral service, visitation or calling hours,

	YES	NO	DON'T RECALL
was the casket present?.	☐	☐	☐
was the casket open?	☐	☐	☐

10. What was the casket made of?

Wood. . . . . . ☐   Precious metal. . . ☐ (copper, bronze)   Other. . . . . ☐

Metal . . . . . . ☐   Fiberglass . . . . . ☐   Don't recall . . . . ☐

200

11. Did the funeral involve attending a service at the cemetery?

Yes, and I attended . . . . . . ☐   No, the funeral did not include that . . ☐

Yes, but I did not attend . . . ☐   Don't recall . . . . ☐

12. How was the body of the deceased put to rest?

Burial in the ground . . . . . ☐   Burial at sea . . . . ☐

Cremation, burial in the ground. . . . . ☐   Donation to science. . . . . ☐

Cremation, other than burial in the ground. . . . . . . ☐   Other. . . . . ☐

Entombment above ground . ☐   Don't recall . . . . ☐

13. What was your reaction to this funeral?

It was very well done . . . . . ☐   It was somewhat poorly done . . . . . . ☐

It was reasonably well done . ☐   It was very poorly done . . . . ☐

It did not stand out one way or another. . . . . ☐   Don't recall or no opinion . . . . ☐

SECTION 2

We are now interested in what experiences you personally have had in making funeral arrangements.

1. In the PAST 5 YEARS, how many funeral arrangements at a funeral home have you made for any of the people listed below? That is, for each category of people, how many funerals did you make or help make the major decisions about? (On each line in column 1 below please write the number of funeral arrangements you have made for people in that category. If you have made none, please write "0" on that line.)

2. In the second column below, please "X" which ONE of the funeral arrangements you made MOST RECENTLY.

	Number of Funerals Arranged	Most Recently Arranged (Please "X" only 1 box)
Spouse	___ . . .	☐
Mother	___ . . .	☐
Father	___ . . .	☐
Son or daughter	___ . . .	☐
Brother or sister.	___ . . .	☐
Grandparent.	___ . . .	☐
Other relative	___ . . .	☐
Close personal friend	___ . . .	☐
Acquaintance or other person	___ . . .	☐

Please answer the following questions for the funeral you most recently arranged. If you have NOT made such arrangements, skip to Section 3.

3. How much information had the deceased left about the kind of funeral wanted?

Left detailed information . . . . ☐   Wishes were not known . . . . ☐

General wishes were known . . . ☐   Don't recall . . . . ☐

4. What would you say was your role in making the funeral arrangements?

Primary decision maker. . . . . . ☐   Participated, but others had a more important role in the decision making . ☐

Participated equally with others in decision making . . . . ☐   Participated by carrying out pre-existing detailed plans . . . . ☐

5. How many people accompanied you to the funeral home to make the arrangements?

0 . . . . ☐   5-7 . . . . ☐

1 . . . . ☐   More than 8 . . . . ☐

2-4 . . . . ☐   Don't recall . . . . ☐

6. Which one(s) of those who accompanied you to the funeral home had a role in the decisionmaking? (Please check all that apply.)

Close relatives of the deceased. . ☐   Attorney. . . . . ☐

Other relatives or friends. . . . . ☐   Other. . . . . ☐

Clergyman . . . . ☐   Don't recall . . . . ☐

7. Did anyone else, besides those you indicated above, have a role in deciding about these arrangements? (Please check all that apply.)

Yes, my clergyman . . . . . . ☐   Yes, the funeral director . . . . ☐

Yes, my immediate family . . ☐   Yes, a memorial society . . . . ☐

Yes, other relatives . . . . . . ☐   Yes, others. . . . . ☐

Yes, friend(s) . . . . ☐   No . . . . ☐

Yes, an attorney. . . . . ☐   Don't recall . . . . ☐

8. In making these funeral arrangements, did you call or go to more than one funeral home to compare services and prices?

Yes . . . . ☐   Don't recall . . . . ☐

No . . . . ☐

SECTION 3

We now turn to questions about planning funerals ahead of time.

202

1. Have any of the following people in your family discussed with other family members what kinds of funeral arrangements they wish to have for themselves? (Please check the box that applies for each person. If you are not married or have no family members, please check the "not applicable" box in that column.)

	You	Your Spouse	Your Parents and/or Other Family Members
Yes, arrangements have been discussed.........	☐	☐	☐
No, arrangements have not been discussed	☐	☐	☐
Not applicable...................		☐	☐

If you checked "no" for ALL of the above, please skip to Question 4.

2. What is the primary way the wishes of these people have been made known? (Please check only 1 box for each column below. If you are not married or have no family members, please check the "not applicable" box in that column.)

	You	Your Spouse	Parents and/or Other Family Members
Through casual comments about general funeral arrangements ...	☐	☐	☐
By discussion at some length of the details involved	☐	☐	☐
By written instructions.......	☐	☐	☐
Through a will.............	☐	☐	☐
They have not made their wishes known	☐	☐	☐
Not applicable.................		☐	☐

3. Which of the following preferences about funeral arrangements has each of these people made known? (Please check all boxes that apply in each column. Use the "not applicable" box if you have no spouse and/or family members.)

	You	Your Spouse	Parents and/or Other Family Members
Whether or not a funeral service should be held	☐	☐	☐
How the body should be put to rest (e.g., burial, cremation, etc.)	☐	☐	☐
What the overall cost should be.	☐	☐	☐
Which funeral home should be used.	☐	☐	☐
Type of casket to be used	☐	☐	☐
Kind of funeral service to be held	☐	☐	☐
They have not made their wishes known	☐	☐	☐
Not applicable.................		☐	☐

203

4. How do you feel about making specific arrangements for your funeral in advance of need at a funeral home?

I already have . . . . ☐   It is not a good idea. . . . . ☐
                                          (PLEASE SKIP TO QUESTION 6.)
I feel that I should, and
probably will . . . . ☐   Undecided or don't care . . . . ☐

I feel that I should, but probably
won't get around to it . . . . . . ☐

5. Would you be willing to pay for the funeral arrangements before they are needed?

Yes, 10% of the cost . . . . . . ☐   Yes, 100% of the cost . . . . ☐

Yes, 10% to 50% of the cost. . ☐   No, I would not be willing to
                                        make any prepayment . . . . ☐
Yes, 50% to 90% of the cost. . ☐

6. Are you aware of any funeral homes in your area that offer pre-need funeral arrangements, either prepaid or not?

Yes, I have heard a lot about this . . . ☐

Yes, I have heard a little about this. . ☐

No, I have heard nothing about this . ☐

7. What are your feelings about being contacted by a funeral home about prearrangement services they offer for any of the following people? (Please check only 1 box in each column.)

	For Yourself	For Your Spouse	For Parents and/or Other Family Members
I would very much like to be contacted	☐	☐	☐
I wouldn't mind being contacted	☐	☐	☐
I would not like to be contacted	☐	☐	☐
Undecided or no opinion. . . .	☐	☐	☐
I have already been contacted	☐	☐	☐
Not applicable.	☐	☐	☐

8. Do any of the following have insurance designed specifically to cover funeral costs? (We mean a policy that can only be used for funeral costs.)

	You	Your Spouse	Your Parents or Other Family Members
Yes	☐	☐	☐
No	☐	☐	☐
Don't know	☐	☐	☐
Not applicable.		☐	☐

204

SECTION 4

The following questions ask about your attitudes about funeral services.

1. What kind of funeral services would you prefer for the following people? (Please check only one box in each column. If you have no spouse and/or family members, please check the "not applicable" box in that column.)

	For You	For Your Spouse	For Your Parents or Other Family Members
A funeral service that stands out	☐	☐	☐
A funeral service typical for my family and friends	☐	☐	☐
An inexpensive, no frills funeral service.	☐	☐	☐
No funeral service.	☐	☐	☐
Undecided or no opinion. . . .	☐	☐	☐
Not applicable.		☐	☐

2. For a funeral of this kind, what would you expect it would cost? (Please write in your estimate in dollars for each of the three kinds of funerals. If you have no spouse and/or family members, please mark "0" in that line below.)

For Yourself	For Your Spouse	For Your Parents or Other Family Members
$ _____	$ _____	$ _____
(write in estimate)	(write in estimate)	(write in estimate)

3. How much total time should be devoted to speakers' comments (i.e., sermons, eulogies, and other remarks) during a funeral service? (Please check only one.)

Only a few minutes (5 to 10) . . ☐   At least 30 minutes or more. . . . . ☐

Several minutes (15 to 20). . . . ☐   Undecided or no opinion. . . . . ☐

4. Which of the following arrangements do you prefer?

Have the casket open during the visitation/calling hours/ wake and during the funeral. . . . .☐

Have the casket open during the visitation/calling hours/ wake but closed during the funeral . . . .☐

Have the casket closed during the visitation/calling hours/ wake and the funeral . . . .☐

Not have the casket present at all. . . . .☐

Undecided or no opinion. . . . .☐

205

5. About how many days, in all, should the visitation, calling or wake period AND the funeral service take (not counting the time between the visitation period and the funeral service)? (Please check only ONE.)

1 day . . . . ☐   3 days . . . . ☐

2 days . . . . ☐   4 or more days . . . . ☐

6. Who should attend a funeral service? (Please check only ONE.)

No one, because there should not be a funeral service . . . . ☐

Only immediate relatives. . . . . ☐

Relatives and friends . . . . ☐

Relatives, friends and acquaintances . . . . ☐

There should not be any restrictions on who attends. . . . . ☐

7. If someone dies WHOM YOU KNOW FAIRLY WELL BUT WHO IS NOT A CLOSE FRIEND, would you attend the following? (Please check only ONE box in each column.)

	The Visitation or Calling Hours or Wake		The Funeral Service
I always go.	☐	. . . .	☐
I frequently go	☐	. . . .	☐
I sometimes go	☐	. . . .	☐
I seldom go	☐	. . . .	☐
I never go	☐	. . . .	☐

8. If someone dies WHO IS ONLY AN ACQUAINTANCE, would you attend the following? (Please check only ONE box in each column.)

	The Visitation or Calling Hours or Wake		The Funeral Service
I always go.	☐	. . . .	☐
I frequently go	☐	. . . .	☐
I sometimes go	☐	. . . .	☐
I seldom go	☐	. . . .	☐
I never go	☐	. . . .	☐

SECTION 5

We now turn to questions about funeral homes.

1. Do you have a preferred funeral home, one that you would probably turn to if needed?

Yes . . . . ☐   No . . . . ☐
(PLEASE SKIP TO QUESTION 3.)

206

2. How would you rate that funeral home?

Excellent — satisfactory in every way . . . . ☐

Good — generally satisfactory. . . . . ☐

Fair — generally satisfactory, but some things are not good . . . . ☐

Poor — not satisfactory on several important things . . . . ☐

Bad — very unsatisfactory . . . . ☐

3. When selecting a funeral home, how would you rank the importance of the following factors in making your decision? (Please write a "1" beside the information you consider most important, a "2" beside the information you consider second most important, and so forth until you have put a "5" beside the information you consider least important. Please be sure you rank all 5 kinds of information.)

Prior experience with the funeral home by oneself, family or friends . . . . . . ——

Ethnic or religious affiliation of the funeral home . . . . ——

Funeral director's reputation in the community . . . . ——

Convenience of the funeral firm to one's home . . . . ——

Appearance and "feeling" of the funeral home and staff. . . . . ——

4. Do you think that funeral homes in general should advertise?

No, they should not . . . . ☐

Yes, it is desirable. . . . . ☐
Undecided or no opinion. . . . . ☐ ⟶ Please skip to Question 6

5. What is the primary reason you think they should not advertise? (Please check only ONE box.)

It would be in bad taste . . . . ☐

People don't choose funeral homes by the kind of information
an ad could contain. . . . . ☐

Offerings don't vary that much among funeral homes . . . . ☐

It would add to cost . . . . ☐

Other reason. . . . . ☐

6. If funeral homes were to advertise, how would you rank the importance of each of the following kinds of information in helping you choose a funeral home? (Please write a "1" beside the information you consider most important, a "2" beside the information you consider second most important and so forth until you have put a "5" beside the information you consider least important. Please be sure you rank all 5 kinds of information.)

Appearance and "feeling" of the funeral home and staff. . . . . ——

Characteristics of the funeral home (religious affiliation,
hours, friendliness of staff, personal attention, etc.) . . . . ——

Location of funeral home . . . . ——

Prices. . . . . ——

Types of professional services available (i.e., coordination
of funeral arrangements, driving the limousine, etc.) . . . . ——

207

SECTION 6

This section examines your preferences about caskets.

1. What price of casket would you probably select for each of the following? (Please check only one box in each column. If you are not married and/or have no family members, please check "not applicable" in that column.)

	Casket for Yourself		Casket for Your Spouse		Casket for Parents or Other Family Members
One that is above my income bracket	☐	. . .	☐	. . .	☐
One that is within my income bracket	☐	. . .	☐	. . .	☐
One that is below my income bracket	☐	. . .	☐	. . .	☐
Would not want a casket.	☐	. . .	☐	. . .	☐
Undecided or no opinion.	☐	. . .	☐	. . .	☐
Not applicable.			☐	. . .	☐

2. For a casket of this kind, what would you expect it to cost you? (Please write in your estimates in dollars. If you indicated that you would want no casket for any of the above, or have no spouse and/or family members, please mark "0" in the blank below.)

Casket for Yourself	Casket for Your Spouse	Casket for Your Parents or Other Family Members
_____	_____	_____
(write $ estimate)	(write $ estimate	(write $ estimate)

3. What kind of casket material would you probably select for each of the following, given that each material is within your price range?

	For Yourself		For Your Spouse		For Parents or Other Family Members
Wood.	☐	. . .	☐	. . .	☐
Steel	☐	. . .	☐	. . .	☐
Stainless steel	☐	. . .	☐	. . .	☐
Precious metal (e.g., copper or bronze)	☐	. . .	☐	. . .	☐
Fiberglass	☐	. . .	☐	. . .	☐
No casket	☐	. . .	☐	. . .	☐
Don't know	☐	. . .	☐	. . .	☐
Not applicable.			☐	. . .	☐

4. How much of a difference would what the casket is made of make to you?

It would make a lot of difference to me. . . . . ☐   It would make only a small difference . . . . ☐

It would make some difference to me. . . . . ☐   It would make no difference to me. . . . . ☐

5. How would you rank the importance of the following casket attributes? (Write a "1" beside the attribute you consider most important, a "2" beside the attribute you consider second most important and so forth until you have put an "8" beside the attribute you ranked least important. Please make sure you rank ALL 8 attributes.)

Exterior appearance . . . . _____

Color. . . . . _____

Protection over the years. . . . . _____

Thickness of casket wall . . . . _____

Interior appearance. . . . . _____

Reputation of casket manufacturer. . . . . _____

Quality of construction . . . . _____

Recommendation of funeral director. . . . . _____

6. Please rank the importance of the following meanings or values that a casket provides. (As above, write a "1" beside the one you consider the most important meaning, a "2" beside the one you consider second most important, and so on until you put a "5" beside the one you consider least important. Please be sure you rank all 5 statements.)

Symbol of love and concern for the deceased . . . . _____

Gives protection to the body of the deceased . . . . _____

Provides warmth and beauty during the funeral. . . . . _____

Expresses personality of the deceased . . . . _____

Maintains family tradition and pride . . . . _____

7. If it were possible to save 20% or so by buying a casket from some place other than a funeral home, would you?

Definitely . . . . ☐   Probably not. . . . . ☐

Probably . . . . ☐   Definitely not . . . . ☐

Undecided or no opinion. . . . ☐

8. What is your opinion about using a rental casket for display of the body and then using an inexpensive, plain container for placing the body in its final resting place?

Sounds awful, and I'm totally against it . . . . ☐

Sounds okay for some people but not for me . . . . ☐

Sounds interesting and I might consider it. . . . . ☐

Sounds good and I would want to use a rental casket . . . . ☐

Undecided or no opinion. . . . . ☐

209

SECTION 7

Now we turn briefly to questions about your preferences
for burial versus other alternatives.

1. If is were up to you, what would you probably arrange for each of the following?
(Please check only ONE box in each column.)

	For Yourself	For Your Spouse	For Someone in Your Immediate Family or Close Friend
Burial in the ground	☐	☐	☐
Cremation	☐	☐	☐
Donation to science.	☐	☐	☐
Entombment above the ground . .	☐	☐	☐
Burial at sea	☐	☐	☐
Other.	☐	☐	☐
Undecided or no opinion.	☐	☐	☐

2. If you checked cremation above, what would you like done with the ashes? If you
did not check cremation for any of the above, please skip to Section 8.

	For Yourself	For Your Spouse	For Someone in Your Immediate Family or Close Friend
Scattered on land or sea	☐	☐	☐
Burial in the ground	☐	☐	☐
Entombment above ground (i.e., in a columbarium)	☐	☐	☐
Retained in home.	☐	☐	☐
Undecided or no opinion.	☐	☐	☐

SECTION 8

The following questions ask for your opinions about the pricing and costs of funerals.

1. Funeral costs differ, but what would you estimate to be the average price paid for a
funeral? This would include the casket, facilities and service, but NOT the cemetery
lot or a vault.

$ _____
(write in estimate)

2. What do you THINK this price SHOULD be?

$ _____
(write in estimate)

210

3. Of the price you indicated in Question 1, what percentage do you think is profit for the funeral firm after all costs and expenses are deducted?

_____ %
(write in estimate)

4. What do you THINK the percentage of profit SHOULD be?

_____ %
(write in estimate)

5. When you pay for a funeral, you pay for several different items such as the casket, facilities (building, automobiles, etc.) and professional service. (1) What percentage of that price do you think each of the following items ACTUALLY is? (2) What percentage do you THINK they SHOULD be?

Item	(1) Percent of Total Price	(2) Percent They Should Be
Professional services (coordination of arrangements, etc.) . . .	_____	_____
Facilities (buildings, furnishings, etc.)	_____	_____
Casket	_____	_____
Total MUST equal . . .	100%	100%

6. Compared to medical and hospital care, funeral prices are:

Rising faster . . . . . ☐   Rising about the same. ☐   Rising slower . . . . ☐

7. Compared to the overall cost of living, funeral prices are:

Rising faster . . . . . ☐   Rising about the same. ☐   Rising slower . . . . ☐

8. There are several ways to inform people arranging funerals about the price. Which of the following pricing methods would you prefer, assuming that the total price would be the same with any of the methods?

UNIT PRICING: ONE total price is given which includes the cost of the casket, professional services, and use of the facilities . . . . ☐

FUNCTIONAL PRICING: THREE prices are given: one for the casket, one for the services, and one for the facilities . . . . . ☐

ITEMIZED PRICING: MANY prices are given: for specific items of service (such as embalming, arranging the funeral, etc.) for specific facilities provided (automobiles, visitation room, etc.) and for the casket . . . . ☐

211

9. Suppose an extended payment plan were available from a funeral home that allowed the funeral to be paid for over a 1 to 3 year period after the funeral. Assume the plan is confidentially and professionally handled, and charges the going interest rate for the extended payments. If you were making funeral arrangements, what would be your response to this plan?

I would be almost certain to use the extended payment plan. . . . . ☐

I would probably use the extended payment plan . . . . ☐

Indifferent or don't know. . . . . ☐

I would probably not use the extended payment plan . . . . ☐

I would be almost certain not to use the extended payment plan. . . . . ☐

Supplemental Tables

TABLE 1

How many funerals have you attended in the PAST FIVE YEARS for family members, friends and acquaintances?

		SEX		AGE		EDUCATION			INCOME			REGION					RELIGIOUS			ARRG. FNRL.	
		M	F	Under 45	45 & Over	HS or Less	Some Clge/ More	8000 to 19999	20000 & Over	East	Mid-west	South	West	Rather	Not Very	Yes	No
0	N=	97	82	91	86	73	105		74	71	36	35	47	60	92	87	20	159
	%=	13.2	11.2	15.3	10.0	10.9	13.5		12.4	10.3	10.7	8.2	11.4	21.3	10.7	14.6	4.5	15.5
1-4	N=	437	382	400	408	371	436		333	405	206	237	228	149	424	389	220	599
	%=	59.4	52.3	66.8	47.7	55.5	56.0		56.0	59.0	60.7	55.1	54.5	53.0	49.2	65.1	50.0	58.3
5-9	N=	130	156	78	208	132	151		103	138	64	99	81	42	202	82	114	172
	%=	17.7	21.3	13.0	24.3	19.7	19.3		17.3	20.1	18.9	22.9	19.4	15.1	23.5	13.7	26.0	16.7
10-14	N=	31	53	21	63	45	39		40	35	18	21	30	16	71	13	35	49
	%=	4.2	7.3	3.5	7.4	6.7	5.1		6.8	5.0	5.2	4.8	7.1	5.7	8.3	2.2	7.9	4.8
15-19	N=	16	15	5	26	17	12		13	13	6	15	9	1	23	8	18	13
	%=	2.1	2.1	0.8	3.0	2.5	1.5		2.2	1.9	1.7	3.4	2.1	0.4	2.6	1.3	4.0	1.2
20 or more	N=	25	43	4	64	32	36		32	26	9	24	23	13	50	19	34	35
	%=	3.4	5.9	0.7	7.5	4.7	4.7		5.3	3.7	2.6	5.5	5.5	4.5	5.8	3.1	7.7	3.4
No answer	N=	4	9	4	9	8	5		5	6	7	3	2	1	7	3	3	10
Analyzed	N=	736	731	599	855	669	780		595	687	338	431	417	281	861	597	440	1027
Respondents	%=	100.0	100.1	100.1	99.9	100.0	100.1		100.0	100.0	99.8	99.9	100.0	100.0	100.1	100.0	100.1	99.9

TABLE 2

How many times have you attended visitation/calling hours or wakes in the past 5 years?

		SEX		AGE		EDUCATION		INCOME		REGION				RELIGIOUS		ARRG. FNRL	
		M	F	Under 45	45 & Over	HS or Less	Some Clge/More	8000 to 19999	20000 & Over	East	Mid-west	South	West	Rather	Not Very	Yes	No
0	N=	132	110	147	90	89	149	101	113	29	40	68	104	121	119	42	200
	%=	20.6	17.4	27.4	12.4	15.6	21.8	19.7	18.7	9.5	10.4	19.0	47.5	16.1	23.1	11.5	22.1
1-4	N=	243	247	240	244	196	288	190	248	116	155	144	75	255	233	128	362
	%=	37.9	39.1	44.7	33.8	34.3	42.2	36.9	41.0	37.6	40.1	40.3	34.1	33.9	45.3	35.0	39.9
5-9	N=	122	135	84	172	138	117	98	126	77	93	59	29	172	84	85	173
	%=	19.1	21.4	15.7	23.7	24.2	17.1	19.0	20.9	24.9	24.0	16.6	13.0	22.8	16.3	23.1	19.1
10-14	N=	72	60	39	93	73	57	58	59	39	47	38	7	84	48	42	90
	%=	11.2	9.5	7.3	12.8	12.8	8.3	11.3	9.8	12.7	12.3	10.8	3.1	11.1	9.4	11.5	9.9
15-19	N=	35	17	14	38	20	32	21	23	20	14	18	1	40	12	22	30
	%=	5.5	2.7	2.5	5.3	3.4	4.7	4.0	3.7	6.3	3.5	5.0	0.5	5.3	2.3	5.9	3.4
20 or more	N=	37	62	13	86	56	39	47	36	28	38	30	4	80	19	48	51
	%=	5.8	9.8	2.4	11.9	9.7	5.8	9.2	5.9	8.9	9.7	8.3	1.8	10.7	3.6	13.0	5.7
No answer	N=	99	109	67	141	106	101	85	89	36	47	62	62	116	85	76	132
Analyzed Respondents	N=	641	631	536	723	571	683	515	604	309	386	357	220	752	515	367	905
	%=	100.1	99.9	100.0	99.9	100.0	99.9	100.1	100.0	99.9	100.0	100.0	100.0	99.9	100.0	100.0	100.1

TABLE 3

How many funeral services have you attended in the past 5 years for a spouse?

		SEX		AGE		EDUCATION		INCOME			REGION					RELIGIOUS			ARRG. FNRL.	
		M	F	Under 45	45 & Over	HS or Less	Some Clge/ More	8000 to 19999	20000 & Over	East	Mid-West	South	West	Rather	Not Very	Yes	No				
0	N=	637	614	503	736	577	659	507	611	295	384	357	215	746	496	387	864				
	%=	99.7	94.6	99.2	95.7	96.8	97.6	97.3	99.2	97.7	97.2	96.5	97.3	97.0	97.3	92.2	99.5				
1	N=	2	23	3	22	10	13	10	5	6	9	5	5	14	11	23	2				
	%=	0.3	3.5	0.6	2.9	1.7	1.9	1.9	0.8	2.0	2.3	1.4	2.3	1.8	2.1	5.5	0.2				
X*	N=	—	10	1	9	8	2	4	—	1	2	6	1	7	3	10	—				
	%=	—	1.5	0.2	1.2	1.3	0.3	0.8	—	0.3	0.5	1.6	0.5	0.9	0.6	2.4	—				
R*	N=	—	2	—	2	1	1	—	—	—	—	2	—	2	—	—	2				
	%=	—	0.3	—	0.3	0.2	0.1	—	—	—	—	0.5	—	0.3	—	—	0.2				
Analyzed Respondents	N=	639	649	507	769	596	675	521	616	302	395	370	221	769	510	420	868				
	%=	100.0	99.9	100.0	100.1	100.0	99.9	100.0	100.0	100.0	100.0	100.0	100.1	100.0	100.0	100.1	99.9				

* In this and the following tables "X" denotes the category "Not Applicable" and "R" denotes the category "No Answer".

TABLE 4

How many funeral services have you attended in the past 5 years for your mother or mother-in-law?

		SEX		AGE		EDUCATION		INCOME		REGION					RELIGIOUS			ARRG. FNRL.	
		M	F	Under 45	45 & Over	HS or Less	Some Clge/ More	8000 to 19999	20000 & Over	East	Mid-west	South	West	Rather	Not Very	Yes	No
0	N=	577	567	478	658	527	602	461	547	282	344	333	184	673	462	308	835
	%=	90.3	87.4	94.1	85.6	88.4	89.2	88.6	88.8	93.5	87.0	90.1	83.5	87.4	90.7	73.4	96.3
1	N=	41	53	28	62	41	51	35	55	11	33	22	29	62	32	72	22
	%=	6.4	8.2	5.5	8.1	6.8	7.6	6.7	8.9	3.6	8.2	5.9	13.0	8.1	6.2	17.2	2.5
2	N=	--	1	--	1	--	1	--	1	--	1	--	--	1	--	1	--
	%=	--	0.2	--	0.1	--	0.1	--	0.2	--	0.3	--	--	0.1	--	0.2	--
X	N=	21	26	2	45	28	20	25	13	9	18	13	8	32	16	39	9
	%=	3.3	4.0	0.4	5.9	4.6	2.9	4.7	2.1	2.9	4.5	3.5	3.6	4.1	3.1	9.2	1.0
R	N=	--	2	--	2	1	1	--	--	--	--	2	--	2	--	--	2
	%=	--	0.3	--	0.3	0.2	0.1	--	--	--	--	0.5	--	0.3	--	--	0.2
Analyzed Respondents	N=	639	649	507	769	596	675	521	616	302	395	370	221	769	510	420	868
	%=	100.0	100.1	100.0	100.0	100.0	99.9	100.0	100.0	100.0	100.0	100.0	100.1	100.0	100.0	100.0	100.0

TABLE 5

How many funeral services have you attended in the past 5 years for your father or father-in-law?

		SEX		AGE		EDUCATION		INCOME		REGION				RELIGIOUS		ARRG. FNRL	
		M	F	Under 45	45 & Over	HS or Less	Some Clge/More	8000 to 19999	20000 & Over	East	Mid-west	South	West	Rather	Not Very	Yes	No
0	N=	557	567	446	668	516	591	460	535	264	349	319	192	672	447	303	822
	%=	87.2	87.4	88.0	86.9	86.6	87.6	88.3	86.9	87.3	88.3	86.4	87.0	87.3	87.6	72.1	94.7
1	N=	56	60	50	66	54	62	43	61	26	36	33	21	72	42	93	24
	%=	8.8	9.2	9.9	8.6	9.1	9.2	8.2	9.9	8.8	9.2	8.8	9.4	9.4	8.3	22.0	2.7
2	N=	--	1	1	--	--	1	--	1	--	--	1	--	--	1	1	--
	%=	--	0.2	0.2	--	--	0.1	--	0.2	--	--	0.3	--	--	0.2	0.2	--
X	N=	25	19	10	32	25	20	19	19	12	10	15	8	24	20	24	21
	%=	4.0	2.9	1.9	4.2	4.1	2.9	3.6	3.0	3.9	2.5	4.0	3.6	3.1	3.9	5.6	2.4
R	N=	--	2	--	2	1	1	--	--	--	--	2	--	2	--	--	2
	%=	--	0.3	--	0.3	0.2	0.1	--	--	--	--	0.5	--	0.3	--	--	0.2
Analyzed Respondents	N=	639	649	507	769	596	675	521	616	302	395	370	221	769	510	420	868
	%=	100.0	100.0	100.0	100.0	100.0	99.9	100.1	100.0	100.0	100.0	100.0	100.0	100.1	100.0	99.9	100.0

TABLE 6

How many funeral services have you attended in the past 5 years for a son or daughter?

		SEX		AGE		EDUCATION			INCOME			REGION				RELIGIOUS			ARRG. FNRL.	
		M	F	Under 45	45 & Over	HS or Less	Some Clge/ More	8000 to 19999	20000 & Over	East	Mid-west	South	West	Rather	Not Very	Yes	No
0	N=	625	632	495	750	582	658	509	601	293	386	358	220	755	494	397	861
	%=	97.9	97.4	97.7	97.6	97.7	97.5	97.7	97.6	97.1	97.8	96.8	99.5	98.1	96.9	94.4	99.2
1	N=	10	8	10	8	9	9	8	9	6	6	6	—	7	11	16	2
	%=	1.5	1.2	1.9	1.0	1.5	1.3	1.5	1.4	1.9	1.5	1.6	—	0.9	2.1	3.7	0.2
2	N=	—	1	1	—	—	1	—	1	—	—	—	1	—	1	—	1
	%=	—	0.2	0.2	—	—	0.1	—	0.2	—	—	—	0.5	—	0.2	—	0.1
X	N=	4	5	—	9	4	5	4	4	3	3	3	—	5	4	8	1
	%=	0.6	0.8	—	1.2	0.7	0.7	0.8	0.6	1.0	0.8	0.8	—	0.6	0.8	1.9	0.1
R	N=	—	3	1	2	1	2	—	1	—	—	3	—	3	—	—	3
	%=	—	0.5	0.2	0.3	0.2	0.3	—	0.2	—	—	0.8	—	0.4	—	—	0.3
Analyzed Respondents	N=	639	649	507	769	596	675	521	616	302	395	370	221	769	510	420	868
	%=	100.0	100.1	100.0	100.1	100.1	99.9	100.0	100.0	100.0	100.1	100.0	100.0	100.0	100.0	100.0	99.9

TABLE 7

How many funeral services have you attended in the past 5 years for a brother or sister?

		SEX		AGE		EDUCATION			INCOME			REGION				RELIGIOUS		ARRG. FNRL.	
		M	F	Under 45	45 & Over	HS or Less	Some Clge/ More	8000 to 19999	20000 & Over	East	Mid-west	South	West	Rather	Not Very	Yes	No
0	N=	577	564	494	635	502	623	445	574	269	347	323	202	671	462	352	789
	%=	90.3	86.9	97.5	82.5	84.2	92.4	85.4	93.2	88.9	87.8	87.4	91.5	87.2	90.7	83.8	90.9
1	N=	41	51	10	82	53	38	50	28	23	25	34	11	63	29	33	59
	%=	6.4	7.9	2.0	10.6	9.0	5.7	9.6	4.5	7.5	6.2	9.1	4.9	8.2	5.6	7.8	6.8
2	N=	8	13	--	21	18	1	9	4	4	10	2	5	10	11	13	8
	%=	1.2	2.0	--	2.7	3.0	0.1	1.7	0.6	1.3	2.5	0.5	2.2	1.3	2.1	3.0	0.9
3	N=	2	2	--	4	3	1	2	1	--	2	2	--	3	1	3	1
	%=	0.3	0.3	--	0.5	0.5	0.1	0.4	0.2	--	0.5	0.5	--	0.4	0.2	0.7	0.1
4	N=	2	1	--	3	--	3	--	3	--	2	1	--	3	--	2	1
	%=	0.3	0.2	--	0.4	--	0.4	--	0.5	--	0.5	0.3	--	0.4	--	0.5	0.1
X	N=	10	16	3	23	19	7	15	6	7	10	6	3	18	7	18	8
	%=	1.5	2.5	0.6	3.0	3.2	1.0	2.8	1.0	2.3	2.5	1.6	1.3	2.3	1.4	4.2	0.9
R	N=	--	2	--	2	1	1	--	--	--	--	2	--	2	--	--	2
	%=	--	0.3	--	0.3	0.2	0.1	--	--	--	--	0.5	--	0.3	--	--	0.2
Analyzed Respondents	N=	639	649	507	769	596	675	521	616	302	395	370	221	769	510	420	868
	%=	100.0	100.1	100.1	100.0	100.1	99.8	99.9	100.0	100.0	100.0	99.9	99.9	100.1	100.0	100.0	99.9

TABLE 8

How many funeral services have you attended in the past 5 years for a grandparent?

		SEX		AGE		EDUCATION		INCOME		REGION				RELIGIOUS		ARRG. FNRL.	
		M	F	Under 45	45 & Over	HS or Less	Some Clge/More	8000 to 19999	20000 & Over	East	Mid-west	South	West	Rather	Not Very	Yes	No
0	N=	526	547	329	733	497	563	419	524	259	322	304	188	653	411	368	705
	%=	82.4	84.3	64.8	95.3	83.4	83.4	80.5	85.1	85.7	81.6	82.2	85.3	84.9	80.7	87.6	81.3
1	N=	78	64	117	24	63	75	68	61	28	52	42	20	84	58	39	102
	%=	12.2	9.9	23.1	3.2	10.6	11.1	13.0	9.9	9.1	13.2	11.5	8.8	10.9	11.4	9.4	11.8
2	N=	21	19	35	5	23	18	20	20	10	8	15	8	18	23	8	32
	%=	3.3	2.9	7.0	0.6	3.8	2.6	3.8	3.2	3.2	2.0	4.0	3.6	2.3	4.4	1.9	3.7
3	N=	4	7	11	—	3	8	7	2	5	1	3	2	5	6	1	10
	%=	0.6	1.1	2.1	—	0.5	1.2	1.3	0.3	1.6	0.3	0.8	0.9	0.6	1.2	0.2	1.1
4	N=	2	—	2	—	—	2	2	—	—	2	—	—	—	2	—	2
	%=	0.3	—	0.4	—	—	0.3	0.4	—	—	0.5	—	—	—	0.4	—	0.2
X	N=	8	10	13	5	9	9	5	9	1	10	4	3	8	10	4	14
	%=	1.2	1.5	2.5	0.6	1.5	1.3	0.9	1.4	0.3	2.5	1.1	1.3	1.0	1.9	1.0	1.6
R	N=	—	2	—	2	1	1	—	—	—	—	2	—	2	—	—	2
	%=	—	0.3	—	0.3	0.2	0.1	—	—	—	—	0.5	—	0.3	—	—	0.2
Analyzed Respondents	N=	639	649	507	769	596	675	521	616	302	395	370	221	769	510	420	868
	%=	100.0	100.0	99.9	100.0	100.0	100.0	99.9	99.9	99.9	100.1	100.1	99.9	100.0	100.0	100.1	99.9

TABLE 9

How many funeral services have you attended in the past 5 years for a close personal friend?

		SEX		AGE		EDUCATION		INCOME			REGION				RELIGIOUS			ARRG. FNRL.	
		M	F	Under 45	45 & Over	HS or Less	Some Clge/ More	8000 to 19999	20000 & Over	East	Mid-west	South	West	Rather	Not Very	Yes	No
0	N=	247	274	189	323	225	286	203	249	91	148	167	115	295	219	142	378
	%=	38.6	42.2	37.3	42.1	37.8	42.3	39.0	40.4	30.0	37.4	45.0	52.3	38.4	42.9	33.8	43.6
1	N=	186	142	151	176	142	181	147	149	103	91	76	58	201	128	99	229
	%=	29.2	21.9	29.7	22.9	23.8	26.8	28.1	24.3	34.1	23.1	20.5	26.3	26.1	25.0	23.6	26.4
2	N=	84	77	77	82	70	90	58	90	46	61	38	15	96	65	43	117
	%=	13.1	11.9	15.1	10.6	11.8	13.4	11.2	14.7	15.3	15.4	10.4	6.7	12.4	12.7	10.3	13.5
3	N=	33	38	19	52	32	39	23	44	16	31	17	8	53	16	31	40
	%=	5.2	5.9	3.7	6.8	5.3	5.8	4.4	7.2	5.2	7.8	4.5	3.5	6.9	3.1	7.3	4.7
4	N=	23	25	15	33	31	18	26	18	11	16	13	9	30	19	23	26
	%=	3.6	3.9	2.9	4.4	5.1	2.6	4.9	2.9	3.6	4.0	3.5	4.0	3.8	3.7	5.4	3.0
5	N=	6	15	8	13	9	12	9	11	4	6	9	2	16	5	9	12
	%=	.9	2.3	1.6	1.7	1.5	1.8	1.7	1.8	1.3	1.5	2.4	.9	2.1	1.0	2.1	1.4
6	N=	4	11	5	10	10	5	4	8	4	4	5	2	8	7	8	7
	%	.6	1.7	1.0	1.3	1.7	.7	.8	1.3	1.3	1.0	1.4	.9	1.0	1.3	1.9	.8

TABLE 9 (Continued)

How many funeral services have you attended in the past 5 years for a close personal friend?

		SEX		AGE		EDUCATION		INCOME			REGION				RELIGIOUS			ARRG. FNRL.	
		M	F	Under 45	45 & Over	HS or Less	Some Clge/ More	8000 to 19999	20000 & Over	East	Mid-west	South	West	Rather	Very	Not Very	Yes	No
7	N=	2	—	2	—	—	2	—	2	—	—	2	—	—	—	2	—	2
	%=	.3		.4			.3		.3			.5				.4		.2
8	N=	—	3	1	2	1	2	1	1	1	1	1	—	3	3	—	2	1
	%=		.5	.2	.3	.2	.3	.2	.2	.3	.3	.3		.4	.4		.5	.1
X	N=	50	57	40	87	89	36	44	41	25	33	38	12	58	49	57	50
	%=	7.9	8.8	7.9	8.7	11.6	5.4	8.5	6.7	8.1	8.2	10.4	5.4	7.6	9.6	13.7	5.8
R	N=	—	3	1	2	2	1	—	1	—	—	3	—	2	1	1	2
	%=		.5	.2	.3	.3	.1		.2			.8		.3	.2	.2	.2
Analyzed	N=	639	649	507	769	596	675	521	616	302	395	370	221	769	510	420	868
Respondents	%=	100.0	100.2	100.0	100.1	99.9	99.9	99.9	100.2	99.9	99.9	100.0	100.0	100.0	99.9	100.0	100.0

TABLE 10

How many funeral services have you attended in the past 5 years for a close personal friend?

		SEX		AGE		EDUCATION			INCOME				REGION				RELIGIOUS			ARRG. FNRL.	
		M	F	Under 45	45 & Over	HS or Less	Some Clge/ More	8000 to 19999	20000 & Over	East	Mid-west	South	West	Rather	Not Very	Yes	No
0	N=	344	279	325	290	294	317	251	299	149	172	204	97	323	296	180	443
	%=	53.8	43.0	64.0	37.7	49.3	47.0	48.2	48.6	49.4	43.6	55.1	44.1	42.0	58.0	42.9	51.0
1	N=	97	122	96	122	102	115	81	117	62	70	47	39	137	82	50	169
	%=	15.2	18.8	18.8	15.8	17.1	17.1	15.6	19.1	20.6	17.7	12.8	17.9	17.8	16.1	12.0	19.4
2	N=	66	79	37	108	63	80	61	72	35	45	35	30	87	56	51	94
	%=	10.3	12.2	7.2	14.1	10.6	11.8	11.7	11.7	11.7	11.5	9.4	13.4	11.3	11.0	12.2	10.8
3	N=	33	38	14	57	32	39	35	27	19	20	20	13	49	22	30	41
	%=	5.2	5.9	2.7	7.4	5.3	5.8	6.6	4.3	6.2	5.0	5.3	5.8	6.4	4.3	7.0	4.8
4	N=	14	15	5	24	10	19	6	20	5	11	7	6	25	4	11	18
	%=	2.1	2.3	1.0	3.1	1.6	2.8	1.1	3.2	1.6	2.7	1.9	2.7	3.2	0.8	2.6	2.0
5	N=	33	19	9	43	16	36	17	31	7	17	18	11	38	12	21	31
	%=	5.2	2.9	1.7	5.6	2.7	5.4	3.2	5.1	2.3	4.2	4.8	4.9	5.0	2.3	4.9	3.6
6	N=	2	6	—	8	6	2	5	1	—	3	3	2	7	1	4	4
	%=	0.3	0.9	—	1.0	1.0	0.3	0.9	0.2	—	0.7	0.8	0.9	0.9	0.2	1.0	0.5

(Table 10 continued next page)

TABLE 10 (Continued)

How many funeral services have you attended in the past 5 years for a close personal friend?

		SEX		AGE		EDUCATION		INCOME		REGION				RELIGIOUS		ARRG. FNRL.	
		M	F	Under 45	45 & Over	HS or Less	Some Clge/ More	8000 to 19999	20000 & Over	East	Mid-west	South	West	Rather	Not Very	Yes	No
7	N=	4	3	—	7	2	5	1	3	1	1	3	2	5	2	3	4
	%=	0.6	0.5	—	0.9	0.3	0.7	0.2	0.5	0.3	0.3	0.8	0.9	0.6	0.4	0.7	0.5
8	N=	—	2	1	1	1	1	—	2	—	2	—	—	2	—	2	—
	%=	—	0.3	0.2	0.1	0.2	0.1	—	0.3	—	0.5	—	—	0.3	—	0.5	—
9	N=	14	17	—	31	16	15	17	11	3	16	6	6	26	5	15	16
	%=	2.1	2.6	—	4.0	2.7	2.2	3.2	1.8	1.0	4.0	1.6	2.7	3.3	1.0	3.5	1.8
X	N=	33	67	22	76	54	44	48	33	21	38	26	15	68	31	54	46
	%=	5.2	10.3	4.3	9.9	9.0	6.6	9.1	5.3	6.9	9.7	7.0	6.7	8.9	6.0	12.7	5.4
R	N=	—	2	—	2	1	1	—	—	—	—	2	—	2	—	—	2
	%=	—	0.3	—	0.3	0.2	0.1	—	—	—	—	0.5	—	0.3	—	—	0.2
Analyzed Respondents	N=	639	649	507	769	596	675	521	616	302	395	370	221	769	510	420	868
	%=	100.0	100.0	99.9	99.9	100.0	99.9	99.8	100.1	100.0	99.9	100.0	100.0	100.1	100.1	100.0	100.0

TABLE 11

How many funeral services have you attended in the past 5 years for an acquaintance or other person?

		SEX		AGE		EDUCATION			INCOME		REGION				RELIGIOUS			ARRG. FNRL	
		M	F	Under 45	45 & Over	HS or Less	Some Clge/ More	8000 to 19999	20000 & Over	East	Mid-west	South	West	Rather	Not Very	Yes	No
0	N=	315	317	283	345	318	302	275	273	168	180	171	112	347	280	214	418
	%=	49.2	48.8	55.8	44.9	53.4	44.8	52.9	44.4	55.7	45.7	46.2	50.9	45.1	54.9	51.0	48.1
1	N=	118	94	96	115	88	125	83	116	46	65	63	38	118	92	51	162
	%=	18.5	14.5	18.8	15.0	14.7	18.5	16.0	18.9	15.3	16.4	17.0	17.4	15.4	18.1	12.1	18.6
2	N=	41	63	38	63	48	55	38	55	22	33	30	20	66	35	30	74
	%=	6.4	9.7	7.6	8.2	8.1	8.2	7.2	9.0	7.2	8.2	8.0	9.0	8.6	7.0	7.1	8.5
3	N=	31	28	22	37	23	36	19	35	10	24	15	11	37	23	15	44
	%=	4.9	4.3	4.3	4.9	3.8	5.4	3.6	5.8	3.2	6.0	4.0	4.9	4.7	4.4	3.5	5.1
4	N=	21	20	10	31	18	24	16	23	9	11	13	9	37	4	12	30
	%=	3.3	3.1	1.9	4.1	3.0	3.5	3.0	3.7	2.9	2.7	3.5	4.0	4.9	0.8	2.8	3.4
5	N=	21	20	9	33	18	24	16	22	10	14	12	6	32	10	17	25
	%=	3.3	3.1	1.7	4.2	3.0	3.5	3.0	3.5	3.3	3.5	3.2	2.7	4.1	1.9	4.0	2.8
6	N=	6	11	7	10	5	12	4	7	3	2	12	—	13	4	3	14
	%=	0.9	1.7	1.3	1.3	0.8	1.8	0.8	1.1	1.0	0.5	3.2	—	1.7	0.8	0.7	1.6

(Table 11 continued next page)

TABLE 11 (continued)

How many funeral services have you attended in the past 5 years for an acquaintance or other person?

		SEX		AGE		EDUCATION		INCOME			REGION					RELIGIOUS			ARRG. FNRL.	
		M	F	Under 45	45 & Over	HS or Less	Some Clge/ More	8000 to 19999	20000 & Over	East	Mid-west	South	West	Rather	Not Very	Yes	No
7	N=	2	1	--	3	--	1	3	--	--	--	--	3	3	--	--	3
	%=	0.3	0.2	--	0.4	--	0.1	0.6	--	--	--	--	1.3	0.4	--	--	0.3
8	N=	4	5	3	6	4	5	4	4	1	4	2	2	6	3	3	6
	%=	0.6	0.8	0.6	0.8	0.7	0.7	0.8	0.6	0.3	1.0	0.5	0.9	0.8	0.6	0.7	0.7
9	N=	35	39	15	59	28	44	26	39	15	25	24	11	55	19	35	39
	%=	5.5	6.0	2.9	7.7	4.7	6.6	4.9	6.4	4.9	6.3	6.4	4.9	7.2	3.7	8.2	4.5
X	N=	45	50	26	65	46	47	38	41	19	38	29	9	54	40	42	53
	%=	7.0	7.7	5.0	8.5	7.6	7.0	7.2	6.7	6.2	9.7	7.8	4.0	7.1	7.9	9.9	6.1
R	N=	--	1	--	1	1	--	--	--	--	--	1	--	1	--	--	1
	%=	--	0.2	--	0.1	0.2	--	--	--	--	--	0.3	--	0.1	--	--	0.1
Analyzed	N=	639	649	507	769	596	675	521	616	302	395	370	221	769	510	420	868
Respondents	%=	99.9	100.1	99.9	100.1	100.0	100.1	100.0	100.1	100.0	100.0	100.1	100.0	100.1	100.1	100.0	99.8

TABLE 12

Which ONE of the funerals did you attend MOST RECENTLY?

		SEX		AGE		EDUCATION			INCOME			REGION				RELIGIOUS			ARRG. FNRL.	
		M	F	Under 45	45 & Over	HS or Less	Some Clge/ More	8000 to 19999	20000 & Over	East	Mid-west	South	West	Rather	Not Very	Yes	No
Spouse	N=	—	21	4	17	8	13	9	4	2	7	7	5	11	10	19	2
	%=	—	3.4	0.8	2.4	1.4	2.0	1.8	0.7	0.7	1.9	2.0	2.4	1.5	2.1	4.9	0.2
Mother	N=	27	27	14	38	25	28	18	31	7	23	13	12	34	21	40	15
	%=	4.5	4.4	2.8	5.3	4.4	4.3	3.6	5.3	2.4	6.0	3.7	5.6	4.6	4.3	10.1	1.8
Father	N=	19	19	25	14	16	23	13	20	12	6	12	9	14	23	24	15
	%=	3.2	3.1	5.0	1.9	2.8	3.5	2.6	3.3	4.2	1.6	3.4	4.2	1.9	4.7	6.1	1.8
Son/ Daughter	N=	8	5	3	10	4	9	2	10	6	6	1	—	5	8	11	2
	%=	1.3	0.8	0.6	1.4	0.7	1.4	0.4	1.6	2.1	1.6	0.3	—	0.7	1.6	2.8	0.2
Brother/ Sister	N=	27	28	7	48	37	18	31	12	17	15	18	6	37	18	25	31
	%=	4.5	4.5	1.4	6.7	6.7	2.7	6.4	2.0	5.9	3.9	5.1	2.8	5.1	3.7	6.3	3.7
Grandparent	N=	62	48	93	18	45	63	55	43	17	34	36	24	56	54	11	99
	%=	10.3	7.8	18.9	2.4	8.1	9.7	11.3	7.2	5.9	8.9	10.4	11.2	7.7	11.2	2.8	11.9
Other Relative	N=	181	162	161	179	163	178	132	176	106	101	90	46	195	148	97	245
	%=	29.8	26.3	32.9	24.8	29.3	27.4	27.1	29.4	37.5	26.6	25.6	21.9	26.7	30.6	24.9	29.5
Close Person-al Friend	N=	115	167	71	209	143	132	125	131	56	103	65	57	186	93	89	193
	%=	18.9	27.1	14.5	28.9	25.7	20.4	25.7	22.0	19.8	27.2	18.7	27.3	25.4	19.3	22.8	23.2
Acquaintance/ Other Person	N=	167	139	113	189	115	185	102	171	61	85	108	52	194	108	76	230
	%=	27.6	22.6	23.0	26.2	20.7	28.5	21.0	28.6	21.5	22.4	30.9	24.7	26.5	22.4	19.4	27.7
No answer	N=	33	33	17	47	39	27	33	18	19	18	20	10	38	28	30	36
Analyzed Respondents	N=	606	616	491	722	557	647	488	598	284	377	350	211	732	481	390	831
	%=	100.1	100.0	99.9	100.0	99.8	99.9	99.9	100.1	100.0	100.1	100.1	100.1	100.1	99.9	100.1	100.0

TABLE 13

In the PAST 5 YEARS, how many funeral arrangements at a funeral home have you made for a spouse?

		SEX		AGE		EDUCATION			INCOME		REGION					RELIGIOUS			ARRG. FNRL	
		M	F	Under 45	45 & Over	HS or Less	Some Clge/ More	8000 to 19999	20000 & Over	East	Mid-west	South	West	Rather	Not Very	Yes	No	
0	N=	703	681	590	783	623	744	560	661	333	402	384	266	811	562	347	1037
	%=	95.0	92.0	97.9	90.6	92.1	94.8	93.4	95.5	96.3	92.7	91.5	94.4	93.4	93.6	78.3	100.0
1	N=	4	16	2	18	8	10	6	3	2	8	4	6	8	12	20	--
	%=	0.5	2.2	0.3	2.1	1.2	1.3	1.0	0.4	0.6	1.8	1.0	2.1	0.9	2.0	4.5	--
2	N=	--	1	--	1	1	--	--	1	1	--	--	--	1	--	1	--
	%=	--	0.1	--	0.1	0.1	--	--	0.1	0.3	--	--	--	0.1	--	0.2	--
X	N=	--	16	1	15	11	5	8	2	3	3	7	3	11	5	16	--
	%=	--	2.2	0.2	1.7	1.6	0.6	1.3	0.3	0.9	0.7	1.7	1.1	1.3	0.8	3.6	--
R	N=	33	26	10	47	33	26	26	25	7	21	25	7	38	21	59	--
	%=	4.5	3.5	1.6	5.5	4.9	3.3	4.3	3.7	2.0	4.8	5.9	2.4	4.3	3.6	13.3	--
Analyzed Respondents	N=	740	740	603	864	677	785	599	693	345	434	419	282	868	600	443	1037
	%=	100.0	100.0	100.0	100.0	99.9	100.0	100.0	100.0	100.1	100.0	100.1	100.0	100.0	100.0	99.9	100.0

TABLE 14

In the PAST 5 YEARS, how many funeral arrangements have you made for your mother or mother-in-law?

		SEX		AGE		EDUCATION		INCOME		REGION					RELIGIOUS			ARRG. FNRL.	
		M	F	Under 45	45 & Over	HS or Less	Some Clge/ More	8000 to 19999	20000 & Over	East	Mid-west	South	West	Rather	Not Very	Yes	No		
0	N=	660	635	565	723	586	693	521	610	320	373	355	247	747	538	258	1037		
	%=	89.2	85.8	93.7	83.7	86.6	88.3	87.0	88.1	92.6	86.1	84.7	87.7	86.0	89.7	58.3	100.0		
1	N=	39	50	24	61	37	50	37	47	12	31	24	23	58	30	89	—		
	%=	5.2	6.8	4.0	7.1	5.4	6.4	6.1	6.8	3.4	7.1	5.6	8.1	6.7	4.9	20.1	—		
X	N=	8	29	4	33	21	16	16	10	7	9	16	5	26	11	37	—		
	%=	1.0	3.9	0.7	3.8	3.1	2.0	2.6	1.4	2.0	2.1	3.8	1.8	3.0	1.8	8.3	—		
R	N=	33	26	10	47	33	26	26	25	7	21	25	7	38	21	59	—		
	%=	4.5	3.5	1.6	5.5	4.9	3.3	4.3	3.7	2.0	4.8	5.9	2.4	4.3	3.6	13.3	—		
Analyzed	N=	740	740	603	864	677	785	599	693	345	434	419	282	868	600	443	1037		
Respondents	%=	99.9	100.0	100.0	100.1	100.0	100.0	100.0	100.0	100.0	100.1	100.0	100.0	100.0	100.0	100.0	100.0		

TABLE 15

In the PAST 5 YEARS, how many funeral arrangements have you made for your father or father-in-law?

		SEX		AGE		EDUCATION		INCOME			REGION				RELIGIOUS			ARRG. FNRL.	
		M	F	Under 45	45 & Over	HS or Less	Some Clge/ More	8000 to 19999	20000 & Over	East	Mid-west	South	West	Rather	Not Very	Yes	No
0	N=	647	655	555	736	586	697	540	599	316	372	361	252	759	533	265	1037
	%=	87.4	88.5	92.0	85.2	86.6	88.9	90.1	86.5	91.5	85.9	86.1	89.5	87.5	88.9	59.8	100.0
1	N=	54	41	34	61	42	53	26	57	21	36	19	20	56	37	95	—
	%=	7.3	5.5	5.7	7.1	6.3	6.7	4.3	8.2	6.0	8.4	4.5	7.0	6.5	6.2	21.5	—
2	N=	—	1	1	—	—	1	—	1	—	—	1	—	—	1	1	—
	%=	—	0.1	0.2	—	—	0.1	—	0.1	—	—	0.2	—	—	0.2	0.2	—
6	N=	—	1	1	—	—	1	—	1	—	—	1	—	1	—	1	—
	%=	—	0.1	0.2	—	—	0.1	—	0.1	—	—	0.2	—	0.1	—	0.2	—
X	N=	6	16	2	20	15	7	8	9	2	4	13	3	14	7	22	—
	%=	0.8	2.2	0.3	2.3	2.2	0.9	1.3	1.3	0.6	0.9	3.1	1.1	1.6	1.2	4.9	—
R	N=	33	26	10	47	33	26	26	25	7	21	25	7	38	21	59	—
	%=	4.5	3.5	1.6	5.5	4.9	3.3	4.3	3.7	2.0	4.8	5.9	2.4	4.3	3.6	13.3	—
Analyzed	N=	740	740	603	864	677	785	599	693	345	434	419	282	868	600	443	1037
Respondents	%=	100.0	99.9	100.0	100.1	100.0	100.0	100.0	99.9	1001.	100.0	100.0	100.0	100.0	100.1	99.9	100.0

TABLE 16

In the PAST 5 YEARS, how many funeral arrangements at a funeral home have you made for a son or daughter?

		SEX		AGE		EDUCATION		INCOME	REGION				RELIGIOUS		ARRG. FNRL.		
		M	F	Under 45	45 & Over	HS Clge/More	Some to 19999	8000 20000 & Over	East	Mid-west	South	West	Rather	Not Very	Yes	No	
0	N=	693	703	584	801	633	744	564	654	329	404	390	274	818	567	359	1037
	%=	93.7	95.0	96.9	92.7	93.6	94.9	94.1	94.5	95.2	93.2	93.0	97.2	94.2	94.5	81.1	100.0
1	N=	12	9	9	12	8	13	9	10	7	9	4	1	11	10*	21	—
	%=	1.6	1.2	1.5	1.4	1.2	1.6	1.5	1.4	2.0	2.0	.9	.4	1.3	1.6	4.7	—
X	N=	2	2	—	4	2	2	1	3	3	—	1	—	2	2	4	—
	%=	0.3	0.3	—	0.5	0.3	0.2	0.2	0.4	0.9	—	0.2	—	0.2	0.3	0.9	—
R	N=	33	26	10	47	33	26	26	25	7	21	25	7	38	21	59	—
	%=	4.5	3.5	1.6	5.5	4.9	3.3	4.3	3.7	2.0	4.8	5.9	2.4	4.3	3.6	13.3	—
Analyzed Respondents	N=	740	740	603	864	677	785	599	693	345	434	419	282	868	600	443	1037
	%=	100.1	100.0	100.0	100.1	100.0	100.0	100.1	100.0	100.1	100.0	100.0	100.0	100.0	100.0	100.0	100.0

TABLE 17

In the PAST 5 YEARS, how many funeral arrangements at a funeral home have you made for a brother or sister?

		SEX		AGE		EDUCATION			INCOME			REGION				RELIGIOUS			ARRG. FNRL.	
		M	F	Under 45	45 & Over	HS or Less	Some Clge/ More	8000 to 19999	20000 & Over	East	Mid-west	South	West	Rather	Not Very	Yes	No
0	N=	686	695	591	778	625	738	552	656	337	394	377	273	799	570	343	1037
	%=	92.7	93.9	98.0	90.1	92.3	94.0	92.1	94.8	97.4	90.9	89.9	96.9	92.0	94.9	77.6	100.0
1	N=	17	10	2	25	12	16	15	8	2	12	12	2	21	7	27	—
	%=	2.4	1.4	0.3	2.9	1.7	2.0	2.5	1.1	0.6	2.7	2.8	0.7	2.4	1.1	6.2	—
2	N=	—	2	—	2	2	—	—	2	—	2	—	—	1	1	2	—
	%=	—	0.3	—	0.2	0.3	—	—	0.3	—	0.5	—	—	0.1	0.2	0.5	—
X	N=	4	7	—	11	5	6	7	1	—	5	6	—	10	1	11	—
	%=	0.5	0.9	—	1.3	0.7	0.7	1.2	0.1	—	1.1	1.4	—	1.1	0.2	2.5	—
R	N=	33	26	10	47	33	26	26	25	7	21	25	7	38	21	59	—
	%=	4.5	3.5	1.6	5.5	4.9	3.3	4.3	3.7	2.0	4.8	5.9	2.4	4.3	3.6	13.3	—
Analyzed Respondents	N=	740	740	603	864	677	785	599	693	345	434	419	282	868	600	443	1037
	%=	100.1	100.0	99.9	100.0	99.9	100.0	100.1	100.0	100.0	100.0	100.0	100.0	99.9	100.0	100.1	100.0

TABLE 18

In the PAST 5 YEARS, how many funeral arrangements at a funeral home have you made for a grandparent?

		SEX		AGE		EDUCATION			INCOME			REGION				RELIGIOUS			ARRG. FNRL	
		M	F	Under 45	45 & Over	HS or Less	Some Clge/ More	8000 to 19999	20000 & Over	East	Mid-west	South	West	Rather	Not Very	Yes	No
0	N=	695	699	575	808	629	747	570	647	332	401	389	273	818	565	357	1037
	%=	94.0	94.5	95.4	93.5	92.9	95.2	95.1	93.5	96.0	92.5	92.7	96.8	94.2	94.1	80.7	100.0
1	N=	10	10	12	8	11	9	4	15	5	12	3	–	10	10	20	–
	%=	1.3	1.4	2.0	0.9	1.6	1.1	0.7	2.1	1.4	2.7	0.7	–	1.1	1.6	4.5	–
2	N=	–	2	2	–	1	1	–	2	2	–	–	–	1	1	2	–
	%=	–	0.3	0.3	–	0.1	0.1	–	0.3	0.6	–	–	–	0.1	0.2	0.5	–
X	N=	2	3	4	1	3	2	–	3	–	–	3	2	2	3	5	–
	%=	0.3	0.4	0.7	0.1	0.4	0.3	–	0.4	–	–	0.7	0.7	0.2	0.5	1.1	–
R	N=	33	26	10	47	33	26	26	25	7	21	25	7	38	21	59	–
	%=	4.5	3.5	1.6	5.5	4.9	3.3	4.3	3.7	2.0	4.8	5.9	2.4	4.3	3.6	13.3	–
Analyzed	N=	740	740	603	864	677	785	599	693	345	434	419	282	868	600	443	1037
Respondents	%=	100.1	100.1	100.0	100.0	99.9	100.0	100.1	100.0	100.0	100.0	100.0	99.9	99.9	100.0	100.1	100.0

TABLE 19

In the PAST 5 YEARS, how many funeral arrangements at a funeral home have you made for another relative?

		SEX		AGE		EDUCATION		INCOME			REGION				RELIGIOUS			ARRG. FNRL.	
		M	F	Under 45	45 & Over	HS or Less	Some Clge/ More	8000 to 19999	20000 & Over	East	Mid-west	South	West	Rather	Not Very	Yes	No
0	N=	662	678	572	756	611	711	548	620	319	388	371	262	781	547	303	1037
	%=	89.5	91.6	94.9	87.6	90.3	90.6	91.4	89.5	92.3	89.6	88.5	93.0	90.0	91.2	68.5	100.0
1	N=	33	19	16	36	21	31	17	33	16	17	12	8	34	18	52	--
	%=	4.5	2.6	2.6	4.2	3.1	4.0	2.8	4.8	4.6	3.8	2.8	2.8	4.0	2.9	11.7	--
2	N=	6	3	2	7	5	4	3	6	1	2	5	1	4	5	9	--
	%=	0.8	0.4	0.3	0.8	0.7	0.5	0.5	0.8	0.3	0.4	1.2	0.4	0.5	0.8	2.0	--
3	N=	2	--	--	2	--	2	--	2	--	2	--	--	--	2	2	--
	%=	0.3	--	--	0.2	--	0.2	--	0.3	--	0.4	--	--	--	0.3	0.4	--
4	N=	--	1	--	1	--	1	--	1	--	--	1	--	--	1	1	--
	%=	--	0.1	--	0.1	--	0.1	--	0.1	--	--	0.2	--	--	0.2	0.2	--
5	N=	--	1	--	1	--	1	--	--	--	1	--	--	1	--	1	--
	%=	--	0.1	--	0.1	--	0.1	--	--	--	0.2	--	--	0.1	--	0.2	--
X	N=	4	12	3	13	7	9	6	5	3	3	6	4	10	6	16	--
	%=	0.5	1.6	0.5	1.5	1.0	1.1	1.0	0.7	0.9	0.7	1.4	1.4	1.1	1.0	3.6	--
R	N=	33	26	10	47	33	26	26	25	7	21	25	7	38	21	59	--
	%=	4.5	3.5	1.6	5.5	4.9	3.3	4.3	3.7	2.0	4.8	5.9	2.4	4.3	3.6	13.3	--
Analyzed	N=	740	740	603	864	677	785	599	693	345	434	419	282	868	600	443	1037

TABLE 20

In the PAST 5 YEARS, how many funeral arrangements at a funeral home have you made for a close personal friend?

		SEX		AGE		EDUCATION			INCOME		REGION				RELIGIOUS		ARRG. FNRL.	
		M	F	Under 45	45 & Over	HS or Less	Some Clge/ More	8000 to 19999	20000 & Over	East	Mid-west	South	West	Rather	Not Very	Yes	No
0	N=	697	698	588	796	630	746	562	658	332	404	389	271	808	576	358	1037
	%=	94.2	94.3	97.5	92.1	93.2	95.1	93.7	95.0	96.0	93.2	92.7	96.2	93.1	95.9	80.9	100.0
1	N=	8	10	3	15	7	11	9	8	6	7	5	—	16	2	18	—
	%=	1.0	1.4	0.5	1.7	1.0	1.4	1.5	1.1	1.7	1.6	1.2	—	1.8	0.3	4.0	—
2	N=	—	3	1	2	3	—	2	1	1	1	—	1	2	1	3	—
	%=	—	0.4	0.2	0.2	0.4	—	0.3	0.1	0.3	0.2	—	0.4	0.2	0.2	0.7	—
X	N=	2	3	1	4	3	2	1	—	—	1	1	3	5	—	5	—
	%=	0.3	0.4	0.2	0.5	0.4	0.2	0.2	—	—	0.2	0.2	1.0	0.6	—	1.1	—
R	N=	33	26	10	47	33	26	26	25	7	21	25	7	38	21	59	—
	%=	4.5	3.5	1.6	5.5	4.9	3.3	4.3	3.7	2.0	4.8	5.9	2.4	4.3	3.6	13.3	—
Analyzed Respondents	N=	740	740	603	864	677	785	599	693	345	434	419	282	868	600	443	1037
	%=	100.0	100.0	100.0	100.0	99.9	100.0	100.0	99.9	100.0	100.0	100.0	100.0	100.0	100.0	100.0	100.0

TABLE 21

In the PAST 5 YEARS, how many funeral arrangements at a funeral home have you made for an acquaintance or other person?

		SEX		AGE		EDUCATION		INCOME		REGION				RELIGIOUS		ARRG. FNRL.	
		M	F	Under 45	45 & Over	HS or Less	Some Clge/ More	8000 to 19999	20000 & Over	East	Mid-west	South	West	Rather	Not Very	Yes	No
0	N=	703	710	588	813	637	757	572	662	336	411	395	272	827	575	376	1037
	%=	95.0	95.9	97.5	94.2	94.2	96.5	95.4	95.6	97.2	94.8	94.1	96.5	95.2	95.8	84.9	100.0
1	N=	4	2	4	2	4	2	2	4	3	1	—	2	2	4	6	—
	%=	0.5	0.3	0.6	0.2	0.6	0.2	0.3	0.6	0.9	0.2	—	0.7	0.2	0.6	1.3	—
2	N=	—	1	—	1	1	—	—	1	—	1	—	—	1	—	1	—
	%=	—	0.1	—	0.1	0.1	—	—	0.1	—	0.2	—	—	0.1	—	0.2	—
X	N=	—	1	1	—	1	—	—	—	—	—	—	1	1	—	1	—
	%=	—	0.1	0.2	—	0.1	—	—	—	—	—	—	0.4	0.1	—	0.2	—
R	N=	33	26	10	47	33	26	26	25	7	21	25	7	38	21	59	—
	%=	4.5	3.5	1.6	5.5	4.9	3.3	4.3	3.7	2.0	4.8	5.9	2.4	4.3	3.6	13.3	—
Analyzed Respondents	N=	740	740	603	864	677	785	599	693	345	434	419	282	868	600	443	1037
	%=	100.0	99.9	99.9	100.0	99.9	100.0	100.0	100.0	100.1	100.0	100.0	100.0	99.9	100.0	99.9	100.0

TABLE 22

Which ONE of the funeral arrangements did you make MOST RECENTLY?

		SEX		AGE		EDUCATION		INCOME		REGION				RELIGIOUS		ARRG. FNRL.	
		M	F	Under 45	45 & Over	HS or Less	Some Clge/More	8000 to 19999	20000 & Over	East	Mid-west	South	West	Rather	Not Very	Yes	No
Spouse	N=	2	27	3	26	16	13	12	5	5	9	7	8	16	13	29	—
	%=	0.3	3.9	0.5	3.2	2.5	1.7	2.1	0.8	1.5	2.2	1.8	2.9	2.0	2.3	8.0	—
Mother	N=	35	54	25	60	43	44	37	41	14	27	28	21	63	25	89	—
	%=	5.0	7.7	4.2	7.5	6.7	5.9	6.5	6.3	4.1	6.6	7.2	7.6	7.7	4.3	24.5	—
Father	N=	45	39	30	53	38	45	20	53	22	25	19	19	43	37	84	—
	%=	6.4	5.6	5.2	6.7	6.1	6.0	3.5	8.0	6.4	6.1	4.9	6.8	5.3	6.5	23.0	—
Son/ Daughter	N=	14	9	9	14	9	14	10	12	10	8	4	1	11	12	23	—
	%=	1.9	1.3	1.5	1.7	1.4	1.8	1.7	1.8	2.9	1.9	1.0	0.4	1.3	2.1	6.2	—
Brother/ Sister	N=	17	14	2	29	16	16	18	7	2	17	11	2	23	9	31	—
	%=	2.5	2.0	0.3	3.7	2.5	2.1	3.1	1.0	0.6	4.1	2.8	0.7	2.8	1.6	8.7	—
Grandparent	N=	8	11	11	8	9	10	3	15	7	6	5	1	9	10	19	—
	%=	1.1	1.6	1.8	1.0	1.4	1.3	0.5	2.2	2.1	1.5	1.3	0.4	1.1	1.7	5.2	—
Other Relative	N=	39	30	20	49	30	39	21	41	15	19	24	12	40	28	69	—
	%=	5.6	4.3	3.3	6.2	4.7	5.2	3.7	6.2	4.4	4.6	6.1	4.3	4.9	5.0	19.0	—
Close Person- al Friend	N=	6	10	3	13	7	9	5	6	3	7	3	3	15	1	16	—
	%=	0.8	1.4	0.5	1.6	1.1	1.2	0.9	0.9	0.9	1.7	0.8	1.1	1.8	0.2	4.4	—
Acquaintance/ Other Person	N=	2	2	2	2	2	2	2	2	1	1	—	2	2	2	4	—
	%=	0.3	0.3	0.3	0.3	0.3	0.3	0.4	0.3	0.3	0.2	—	0.7	0.2	0.3	1.1	—
Have Never Arranged a Funeral	N=	532	505	485	544	465	557	438	480	258	287	286	207	595	434	—	1037
	%=	76.1	72.0	82.3	68.1	73.3	74.4	77.6	72.5	76.8	71.0	74.1	75.3	72.8	76.0	—	100.0
No Answer	N=	41	39	13	65	42	35	35	30	10	30	33	7	50	29	80	—
Analyzed Respondents	N=	699	701	590	799	634	749	565	662	336	404	386	275	818	571	363	1037
	%=	100.0	100.1	99.9	100.0	100.0	99.9	100.0	100.0	100.0	99.9	100.0	100.2	99.9	100.0	100.1	100.0

TABLE 23

Have you discussed with other family members what kind of funeral arrangements you wish for yourself?

		SEX		AGE		EDUCATION		INCOME		REGION				RELIGIOUS		ARRG. FNRL.	
		M	F	Under 45	45 & Over	HS or Less	Some Clge/ More	8000 to 19999	20000 & Over	East	Mid-west	South	West	Rather	Not Very	Yes	No
Yes, arrangements have been discussed	N=	303	273	205	363	240	330	232	272	105	150	182	139	337	230	212	364
	%=	49.2	47.2	40.1	54.0	44.5	51.5	46.8	48.8	40.0	42.0	53.4	59.3	48.8	46.6	55.2	44.9
No, arrangements haven't been discussed	N=	313	306	306	309	299	311	264	285	158	207	159	95	353	264	172	447
	%=	50.8	52.8	59.9	46.0	55.5	48.5	53.2	51.2	60.0	58.0	46.6	40.7	51.2	53.4	44.8	55.1
No answer	N=	124	161	92	192	138	143	104	135	83	77	78	47	178	106	59	226
Analyzed Respondents	N=	616	579	511	872	538	642	496	557	263	356	341	234	690	494	383	811
	%=	100.0	100.0	100.0	100.0	100.0	100.0	100.0	100.0	100.0	100.0	100.0	100.0	100.0	100.0	100.0	100.0

TABLE 24

Has your spouse discussed with other family members what kind of funeral arrangements he or she wants for him or herself?

		SEX		AGE		EDUCATION		INCOME		REGION				RELIGIOUS		ARRG. FNRL	
		M	F	Under 45	45 & Over	HS or Less	Some Clge/ More	8000 to 19999	20000 & Over	East	Mid-west	South	West	Rather	Not Very	Yes	No
Yes, arrangements have been discussed	N=	305	216	179	338	219	300	215	250	101	140	154	127	303	210	194	327
	%=	50.2	40.1	36.1	52.9	42.7	48.1	45.9	45.5	38.9	41.7	48.1	54.3	46.2	43.6	54.6	41.3
No, arrangements haven't been discussed	N=	297	272	294	271	270	293	230	282	145	180	150	95	319	248	143	426
	%=	48.9	50.5	59.3	42.4	52.7	46.9	49.2	51.4	55.7	53.8	46.9	40.6	48.7	51.4	40.4	53.8
Not applicable	N=	6	51	23	30	24	31	23	17	14	15	16	12	33	24	18	39
	%=	1.0	9.5	4.6	4.7	4.7	5.0	4.9	3.1	5.4	4.5	5.0	5.1	5.0	5.0	5.1	4.9
No answer	N=	132	201	106	225	165	161	131	143	86	99	100	48	213	118	88	245
Analyzed Respondents	N=	608	539	496	639	512	624	468	550	260	334	320	233	655	482	355	792
	%=	100.1	100.1	100.0	100.0	100.1	100.0	100.0	100.0	100.0	100.0	100.0	100.0	99.9	100.0	100.1	100.0

TABLE 25

Have your parents and/or other family members discussed with
other family members what kinds of funeral arrangements they would want for themselves?

		SEX		AGE		EDUCATION		INCOME			REGION				RELIGIOUS			ARRG. FNRL.	
		M	F	Under 45	45 & Over	HS or Less	Some Clge/ More	8000 to 19999	20000 & Over	East	Mid-west	South	West	Rather	Not Very	Yes	No	Yes	No
Yes, arrangements have been discussed	N=	196	201	201	188	146	249	148	212	85	101	113	98	215	178	130	267		
	%=	38.4	40.0	40.4	37.4	33.2	44.2	37.2	42.1	36.7	33.3	41.2	48.1	38.4	39.9	42.5	37.8		
No, arrangements haven't been discussed	N=	291	262	291	258	273	273	226	266	132	186	142	93	310	241	146	407		
	%=	57.0	52.2	58.4	51.4	62.1	48.5	56.8	52.8	57.3	61.1	51.6	46.0	55.3	54.1	47.8	57.6		
Not applicable	N=	23	39	6	56	21	41	24	25	14	17	20	12	36	27	30	33		
	%=	4.6	7.8	1.2	11.2	4.8	7.3	6.0	5.1	6.0	5.5	7.2	5.9	6.3	6.0	9.7	4.6		
No answer	N=	229	238	104	361	236	221	201	190	115	129	144	79	307	154	137	330		
Analyzed Respondents	N=	511	502	498	503	440	564	398	503	230	304	275	203	561	446	306	707		
	%=	100.0	100.0	100.0	100.0	100.1	100.0	100.0	100.0	100.0	99.9	100.0	100.0	100.0	100.0	100.0	100.0		

TABLE 26

How do you feel about making specific arrangements for your funeral in advance of need at a funeral home?

		SEX		AGE		EDUCATION			INCOME			REGION				RELIGIOUS			ARRG. FNRL	
		M	F	Under 45	45 & Over	HS or Less	Some Clge/ More	8000 to 19999	20000 & Over	East	Mid-west	South	West	Rather	Not Very	Yes	No
I already have	N=	56	61	18	96	56	56	59	34	13	27	37	41	72	42	49	68
	%=	8.7	9.7	3.3	13.2	9.5	8.4	11.2	5.8	4.4	7.0	10.2	16.7	9.8	8.0	12.1	7.8
I feel I should and probably will	N=	192	205	160	236	170	225	169	188	69	121	126	81	254	143	137	260
	%=	29.7	32.5	29.6	32.4	28.7	33.6	32.0	31.9	23.5	32.1	35.3	32.7	34.6	26.9	33.5	30.0
I feel I should but probably won't get to it	N=	202	192	195	197	188	206	164	185	100	125	106	63	225	166	108	286
	%=	31.2	30.5	36.2	27.1	31.8	30.7	31.1	31.3	34.2	33.0	29.5	25.6	30.6	31.4	26.3	33.0
It's not a good idea	N=	64	63	56	69	72	55	59	56	43	31	34	19	58	69	32	96
	%=	9.9	10.0	10.4	9.5	12.2	8.2	11.2	9.5	14.8	8.3	9.4	7.5	7.9	13.0	7.7	11.0
Undecided/ no opinion	N=	132	109	110	129	106	128	76	127	68	74	56	43	126	110	84	158
	%=	20.4	17.3	20.5	17.7	17.8	19.1	14.4	21.5	23.2	19.5	15.6	17.4	17.2	20.7	20.4	18.2
No answer	N=	93	110	64	137	84	115	73	102	52	56	61	34	132	70	33	170
Analyzed Respondents	N=	647	630	539	726	593	670	527	590	293	378	358	247	736	530	409	867
	%=	99.9	100.0	100.0	99.9	100.0	100.0	99.9	100.0	100.1	99.9	100.0	99.9	100.1	100.0	100.0	100.0

TABLE 27

Are you aware of any funeral homes in your area that offer pre-need arrangements, either prepaid or not?
Would you be willing to pay for the funeral arrangements before they are needed?

		SEX		AGE		EDUCATION			INCOME		REGION				RELIGIOUS			ARRG. FNRL	
		M	F	Under 45	45 & Over	HS or Less	Some Clge/ More	8000 to 19999	20000 & Over	East	Mid-west	South	West	Rather	Not Very	No	Yes	No		
Yes, 10% of cost	N=	45	40	44	40	40	42	35	37	11	34	25	15	49	34	54	31	54		
	%=	7.7	7.1	9.2	6.2	7.8	6.9	7.6	7.1	4.4	10.0	7.6	6.5	7.3	7.5	7.1	8.2	7.1		
Yes, 10-50% of cost	N=	66	61	49	76	54	73	48	68	16	31	54	27	75	52	81	46	81		
	%=	11.4	10.9	10.3	11.6	10.5	11.9	10.4	12.8	6.3	8.9	16.8	11.7	11.1	11.4	10.5	12.4	10.5		
Yes, 50-90% of cost	N=	27	26	28	26	24	29	23	18	10	14	20	10	30	23	29	25	29		
	%=	4.7	4.6	5.7	3.9	4.6	4.8	4.9	3.3	3.9	4.0	6.2	4.3	4.5	5.0	3.7	6.6	3.7		
Yes, 100% of cost	N=	49	83	47	84	55	76	60	53	16	25	37	54	79	49	90	42	90		
	%=	8.4	14.8	9.9	12.9	10.7	12.5	12.9	10.1	6.3	7.2	11.4	23.9	11.8	10.8	11.7	11.1	11.7		
No, I wouldn't be willing to make any prepayment	N=	394	350	312	425	344	388	300	353	197	239	186	122	439	299	513	231	513		
	%=	67.9	62.5	64.9	65.3	66.4	63.8	64.2	66.7	79.0	69.8	58.0	53.6	65.2	65.3	66.9	61.8	66.9		
No answer	N=	2	7	2	7	2	6	1	5	1	4	3	1	5	4	5	4	5		
Analyzed Respondents	N=	581	560	481	650	518	609	466	529	249	343	322	228	673	457	767	374	767		
	%=	100.1	99.9	100.0	99.9	100.0	99.9	100.0	100.0	99.9	99.9	100.0	100.0	99.9	100.0	99.9	100.1	99.9		

TABLE 28

What are your feelings about being contacted by a funeral home about prearrangement services they offer for yourself?

		SEX		AGE		EDUCATION		INCOME			REGION					RELIGIOUS			ARRG. FNRL.	
		M	F	Under 45	45 & Over	HS or Less	Some Clge/ More	8000 to 19999	20000 & Over	East	Mid-west	South	West	Rather	Not Very	Yes	No				
Would like very much to be contacted	N=	14	12	13	13	14	12	8	12	7	6	11	2	14	12	14	12				
	%=	1.9	1.7	2.2	1.6	2.2	1.6	1.4	1.8	2.1	1.4	2.7	0.8	1.7	2.1	3.3	1.2				
Wouldn't mind being contacted	N=	70	75	56	89	77	64	68	52	30	48	44	23	94	49	42	102				
	%=	9.8	10.7	9.8	10.7	12.1	8.4	11.8	7.8	8.9	11.5	11.0	8.8	11.3	8.7	10.2	10.3				
Wouldn't like to be contacted	N=	410	385	344	443	320	465	305	407	200	244	195	156	467	320	238	557				
	%=	57.7	54.8	60.1	53.6	50.3	61.3	52.8	61.2	60.3	58.2	48.2	60.6	56.3	56.0	57.1	55.9				
Undecided/ no opinion	N=	175	180	140	209	185	168	156	155	94	99	120	42	194	159	91	264				
	%=	24.6	25.6	24.4	25.3	29.0	22.2	27.0	23.4	28.5	23.5	29.6	16.4	23.3	27.9	21.8	26.5				
Have already been contacted	N=	43	50	20	73	41	50	41	38	1	23	35	35	62	30	32	61				
	%=	6.0	7.1	3.4	8.8	6.4	6.6	7.0	5.8	0.3	5.4	8.5	13.5	7.5	5.3	7.6	6.1				
No answer	N=	29	38	30	37	41	25	22	28	14	14	15	25	38	30	27	41				
Analyzed Respondents	N=	711	702	573	826	636	759	578	664	332	420	404	257	830	571	416	997				
	%=	100.0	99.9	99.9	100.0	100.0	100.1	100.0	100.0	100.1	100.0	100.0	100.1	100.1	100.0	100.0	100.0				

TABLE 29

What are your feelings about being contacted by a funeral home about prearrangement services they offer for your spouse?

		SEX		AGE		EDUCATION			INCOME				REGION				RELIGIOUS			ARRG. FNRL.	
		M	F	Under 45	45 & Over	HS or Less	Some Clge/ More	8000 to 19999	20000 & Over	East	Mid-west	South	West	Rather	Not Very	Yes	No
Would like very much to be contacted	N=	14	8	10	12	12	10	9	8	4	3	14	1	13	9	13	9
	%=	2.0	1.3	1.7	1.6	2.0	1.4	1.6	1.2	1.2	0.7	3.8	0.4	1.7	1.6	3.4	0.9
Wouldn't mind being contacted	N=	64	59	52	71	61	60	55	50	23	45	33	23	83	38	32	92
	%=	9.2	9.3	9.2	9.4	10.4	8.3	10.3	7.6	7.2	11.4	9.0	8.8	10.7	7.1	8.3	9.6
Wouldn't like to be contacted	N=	385	321	321	378	277	418	268	377	176	214	172	144	411	288	205	500
	%=	55.3	50.5	56.7	50.4	47.1	57.8	49.8	57.6	56.1	53.8	47.4	55.9	52.9	52.9	54.1	52.6
Undecided/ no opinion	N=	173	149	137	181	164	156	143	149	89	94	100	39	169	151	76	246
	%=	24.9	23.4	24.2	24.1	27.8	21.6	26.6	22.7	28.5	23.6	27.4	15.3	21.7	27.8	20.0	25.9
Have already been contacted	N=	35	36	15	56	31	38	32	34	—	21	22	29	50	21	24	47
	%=	5.0	5.7	2.6	7.5	5.2	5.3	5.9	5.3	—	5.2	6.0	11.1	6.5	3.8	6.2	5.0
Not applicable	N=	25	63	32	53	45	42	31	36	22	21	24	22	51	38	31	58
	%=	3.6	9.9	5.6	7.0	7.6	5.8	5.7	5.6	7.0	5.3	6.5	8.5	6.5	6.9	8.1	6.0
No answer	N=	45	104	36	113	87	60	62	38	32	37	56	25	92	55	64	85
Analyzed Respondents	N=	695	636	567	751	589	724	537	654	314	397	364	257	776	545	379	952
	%=	100.0	100.1	100.0	100.0	100.1	100.2	99.9	100.0	100.0	100.0	100.1	100.0	100.0	100.1	100.1	100.0

TABLE 30

What are your feelings about being contacted by a funeral home about prearrangement services they offer for parents and/or other family members?

		SEX		AGE		EDUCATION		INCOME		REGION				RELIGIOUS		ARRG. FNRL	
		M	F	Under 45	45 & Over	HS or Less	Some Clge/More	8000 to 19999	20000 & Over	East	Mid-west	South	West	Rather	Not Very	Yes	No
Would like very much to be contacted	N=	14	7	12	9	12	9	12	8	4	11	5	1	12	9	8	13
	%=	2.2	1.2	2.1	1.5	2.3	1.3	2.6	1.3	1.3	3.1	1.6	0.4	1.8	1.7	2.5	1.5
Wouldn't mind being contacted	N=	47	39	49	36	38	44	38	40	19	23	29	16	54	32	24	62
	%=	7.7	6.9	8.8	6.0	7.5	6.7	8.2	6.6	6.4	6.5	9.3	6.9	8.2	6.2	7.6	7.2
Wouldn't like to be contacted	N=	320	295	322	288	241	367	225	336	154	197	139	126	349	261	162	453
	%=	52.9	51.9	57.3	48.1	48.0	55.7	49.3	55.3	52.7	56.3	45.2	55.9	52.9	51.6	52.0	52.6
Undecided/ no opinion	N=	138	145	135	144	135	146	117	134	87	80	74	41	149	133	64	219
	%=	22.8	25.5	24.1	24.0	27.0	22.1	25.7	22.1	30.0	22.9	24.1	18.3	22.6	26.3	20.5	25.4
Have already been contacted	N=	23	24	12	35	22	26	20	22	3	9	19	17	30	18	16	32
	%=	3.8	4.2	2.1	5.9	4.3	3.9	4.3	3.6	1.0	2.5	6.1	7.4	4.5	3.5	5.0	3.7
Not applicable	N=	64	58	32	87	54	68	45	68	25	30	42	25	66	54	38	84
	%=	10.6	10.2	5.6	14.5	10.8	10.3	9.9	11.1	8.4	8.7	13.7	11.0	10.0	10.7	12.3	9.7
No answer	N=	134	172	41	265	175	126	142	85	54	84	112	56	208	95	131	175
Analyzed Respondents	N=	606	568	561	599	502	659	457	607	291	350	308	225	660	505	311	862
	%=	100.0	99.9	100.0	100.0	99.9	100.0	100.0	100.0	99.8	100.0	100.0	99.9	100.0	100.0	99.9	100.1

TABLE 31

What kind of funeral services would you prefer for yourself?

		SEX		AGE		EDUCATION		INCOME		REGION				RELIGIOUS		ARRG. FNRL.	
		M	F	Under 45	45 & Over	HS or Less	Some Clge/ More	8000 to 19999	20000 & Over	East	Mid-west	South	West	Rather	Not Very	Yes	No
A funeral service that stands out	N=	12	9	14	5	13	8	11	8	3	5	10	3	9	12	9	12
	%=	1.6	1.3	2.3	0.6	2.0	1.0	1.8	1.2	0.9	1.2	2.4	1.1	1.1	2.0	2.1	1.2
A funeral service typical for my family and friends	N=	229	255	197	283	240	234	210	220	92	190	131	71	326	158	198	286
	%=	31.3	35.9	33.5	33.7	36.8	30.4	35.8	32.4	27.1	45.4	31.9	25.9	38.7	26.9	46.4	28.2
An inexpensive, no frills funeral service	N=	332	303	235	396	284	344	254	298	149	172	202	111	386	239	146	489
	%=	45.4	42.7	40.0	47.1	43.6	44.5	43.2	43.8	44.2	41.1	49.2	40.7	45.8	40.7	34.2	48.2
No funeral service	N=	87	80	73	91	57	110	68	84	46	21	39	61	62	103	39	128
	%=	11.9	11.3	12.4	10.8	8.8	14.3	11.6	12.3	13.6	5.0	9.6	22.3	7.4	17.6	9.2	12.6
Undecided/ no opinion	N=	72	63	69	66	57	76	44	70	48	31	29	27	59	76	34	100
	%=	9.8	8.9	11.7	7.9	8.8	9.8	7.6	10.3	14.2	7.3	7.0	10.0	7.0	12.9	8.1	9.9
No answer	N=	8	30	15	23	25	13	13	14	7	15	8	8	25	13	16	22
Analyzed Respondents	N=	732	710	588	841	652	772	587	679	338	419	411	274	843	587	427	1015
	%=	100.0	100.1	99.9	100.1	100.0	100.0	100.0	100.0	100.0	100.0	100.1	100.0	100.1	100.1	100.0	100.1

TABLE 32

What kind of funeral services would you prefer for your spouse?

		SEX		AGE		EDUCATION			INCOME			REGION					RELIGIOUS			ARRG. FNRL.	
		M	F	Under 45	45 & Over	HS or Less	Some Clge/ More	8000 to 19999	20000 & Over	East	Mid-west	South	West	Rather	Not Very	Yes	No
A funeral service that stands out	N=	14	13	17	10	14	13	12	12	5	5	12	5	20	7	14	13
	%=	1.9	2.0	2.9	1.2	2.2	1.7	2.1	1.8	1.5	1.2	3.1	1.8	2.4	1.2	3.5	1.3
A funeral service typical for my family and friends	N=	313	252	243	320	267	290	217	299	114	208	171	71	349	212	191	374
	%=	42.6	38.4	41.8	40.2	43.0	38.6	38.1	44.5	35.5	50.7	43.9	26.5	43.4	37.0	48.6	37.5
An inexpensive, no frills funeral service	N=	266	221	171	312	217	263	218	219	124	133	126	104	296	186	101	386
	%=	36.2	33.7	29.5	39.2	34.9	35.1	38.2	32.6	38.5	32.3	32.5	38.9	36.7	32.3	25.8	38.7
No funeral service	N=	66	55	50	67	45	76	51	60	20	20	28	53	53	66	32	89
	%=	9.0	8.4	8.6	8.4	7.2	10.2	9.0	8.9	6.1	4.8	7.3	19.8	6.6	11.5	8.3	8.9
Undecided/ no opinion	N=	68	52	74	46	50	68	42	62	42	24	32	23	46	74	32	88
	%=	9.3	7.9	12.7	5.8	8.1	9.0	7.4	9.2	13.1	5.8	8.1	8.4	5.8	12.8	8.2	8.8
Not applicable	N=	8	63	26	41	29	40	30	21	17	22	20	12	41	30	22	49
	%=	1.1	9.6	4.5	5.1	4.6	5.3	5.2	3.1	5.3	5.3	5.1	4.5	5.1	5.2	5.6	4.9
No answer	N=	6	84	22	68	55	35	29	20	24	22	30	14	63	26	50	40
Analyzed Respondents	N=	734	656	581	796	622	750	570	673	321	412	389	268	805	574	393	997
	%=	100.1	100.0	100.0	99.9	100.0	99.9	100.0	100.1	100.0	100.1	100.0	99.9	100.0	100.0	100.0	100.1

TABLE 33

What kind of funeral services would you prefer for your parents or other family members?

		SEX		AGE		EDUCATION			INCOME			REGION					RELIGIOUS			ARRG. FNRL	
		M	F	Under 45	45 & Over	HS or Less	Some Clge/ More	8000 to 19999	20000 & Over	East	Mid-west	South	West	Rather	Not Very	Yes	No
A funeral service that stands out	N=	10	13	17	6	12	11	13	7	4	3	8	8	13	10	7	16
	%=	1.5	2.1	2.9	0.9	2.2	1.6	2.6	1.1	1.3	0.8	2.3	3.3	1.8	1.9	2.0	1.7
A funeral service typical for my family and friends	N=	276	276	290	259	239	303	212	293	122	200	151	79	337	210	178	373
	%=	43.3	45.3	50.0	39.8	43.9	44.0	43.1	46.4	40.3	54.8	43.8	33.7	47.6	39.9	52.0	41.3
An inexpensive, no frills funeral service	N=	192	160	151	198	149	201	146	167	94	88	104	66	203	147	67	285
	%=	30.2	26.3	25.9	30.4	27.4	29.2	29.7	26.5	31.1	24.2	30.1	28.3	28.6	28.0	19.5	31.6
No funeral service	N=	35	27	25	31	26	36	27	32	12	12	13	26	26	36	15	47
	%=	5.5	4.4	4.2	4.8	4.7	5.3	5.4	5.1	3.9	3.2	3.7	11.0	3.6	6.9	4.3	5.2
Undecided/ no opinion	N=	80	78	85	71	74	84	54	86	47	36	36	38	67	90	44	113
	%=	12.5	12.8	14.6	10.9	13.5	12.2	11.1	13.6	15.6	10.0	10.3	16.5	9.5	17.1	12.9	12.6
Not applicable	N=	45	55	14	86	46	54	41	46	24	26	34	17	63	33	32	68
	%=	7.0	9.0	2.4	13.2	8.4	7.9	8.2	7.3	7.8	7.0	9.7	7.2	8.9	6.2	9.2	7.5
No answer	N=	103	131	22	212	132	95	108	62	42	68	75	48	159	74	100	134
Analyzed Respondents	N=	637	609	581	651	545	689	492	631	303	366	344	233	709	526	343	903
	%=	100.0	99.9	100.0	100.0	100.1	100.2	100.1	100.0	100.0	100.0	99.9	100.0	100.0	100.0	99.9	99.9

TABLE 34

Which of the following arrangements do you prefer?

		SEX		AGE		EDUCATION			INCOME			REGION				RELIGIOUS			ARRG. FNRL.	
		M	F	Under 45	45 & Over	HS or Less	Some Clge/ More	8000 to 19999	20000 & Over	East	Mid-west	South	West	Rather	Not Very	Yes	No
Casket open during wake/ vstn./calling hours & funeral	N=	181	161	132	206	193	138	161	129	65	107	118	51	191	146	119	223
	%=	24.7	22.2	22.3	24.3	29.4	17.8	27.3	18.7	19.3	25.2	28.4	18.7	22.5	24.6	27.3	21.9
Casket open during wake/ vstn./calling hours but not funeral	N=	252	288	207	332	281	256	224	239	127	196	149	68	359	178	193	348
	%=	34.6	39.8	34.9	39.1	42.6	33.0	38.1	34.7	37.7	45.9	35.9	24.9	42.2	30.1	44.1	34.2
Casket closed during wake/ vstn./calling hours & funeral	N=	115	92	95	107	59	147	75	114	52	49	63	42	125	82	46	160
	%=	15.7	12.7	16.1	12.6	9.0	19.0	12.7	16.6	15.4	11.5	15.1	15.5	14.7	13.8	10.6	15.8
Not have casket present at all	N=	84	82	69	95	47	119	59	100	38	26	34	67	81	83	40	126
	%=	11.4	11.3	11.6	11.2	7.1	15.3	10.1	14.6	11.4	6.0	8.3	24.5	9.5	14.0	9.0	12.4
Undecided/ no opinion	N=	99	101	89	109	79	116	69	106	55	48	51	45	95	103	39	161
	%=	13.6	14.0	15.1	12.8	12.0	14.9	11.8	15.4	16.3	11.3	12.4	16.5	11.2	17.4	9.0	15.8
No answer	N=	10	16	10	16	18	8	12	5	8	7	3	8	17	9	6	20
Analyzed Respondents	N=	730	724	593	848	659	777	588	688	337	427	416	274	851	591	437	1017
	%=	100.0	100.0	100.0	100.0	100.1	100.0	100.0	100.0	100.1	99.9	100.1	100.1	100.1	99.9	100.0	100.1

TABLE 35

About how many days, in all, should the visitation, calling, or wake period and the funeral service take (not counting the time between the visitation period and the funeral service)?

		SEX		AGE		EDUCATION			INCOME			REGION				RELIGIOUS			ARRG. FNRL.	
		M	F	Under 45	45 & Over	HS or Less	Some Clge/ More	8000 to 19999	20000 & Over	East	Mid-west	South	West	Rather	Not Very	Yes	No
1 day	N=	282	252	223	305	210	314	204	280	139	132	140	123	290	244	137	397
	%=	39.5	35.0	37.6	36.9	32.2	41.3	35.1	41.5	41.4	31.1	33.6	47.8	34.3	42.0	31.7	39.6
2 days	N=	285	303	235	351	285	300	247	258	122	186	202	78	358	229	183	406
	%=	40.1	42.1	39.7	42.5	43.5	39.3	42.6	38.2	36.5	43.9	48.6	30.4	42.3	39.5	42.3	40.6
3 days	N=	138	158	129	165	154	140	124	131	70	99	72	54	187	103	109	186
	%=	19.3	21.9	21.7	20.0	23.6	18.4	21.4	19.4	20.9	23.4	17.3	21.0	22.1	17.8	25.3	18.6
4 or more days	N=	8	7	6	5	5	8	5	6	4	7	2	2	11	4	3	12
	%=	1.1	1.0	1.0	0.6	0.8	1.0	0.8	0.9	1.2	1.6	0.5	0.8	1.3	0.7	0.7	1.2
No answer	N=	27	20	9	38	23	23	19	18	11	9	3	25	23	21	11	36
Analyzed Respondents	N=	713	720	594	825	654	762	581	675	335	425	416	257	845	579	432	1001
	%=	100.0	100.0	100.0	100.0	100.1	100.0	99.9	100.0	100.0	100.0	100.0	100.0	100.0	100.0	100.0	100.0

TABLE 36

If someone dies WHOM YOU KNOW FAIRLY WELL BUT WHO IS NOT A CLOSE FRIEND, would you attend the funeral service?

		SEX		AGE		EDUCATION			INCOME			REGION				RELIGIOUS			ARRG. FNRL	
		M	F	Under 45	45 & Over	HS or Less	Some Clge/ More	20000 & Over	8000 to 19999	East	Mid-west	South	West	Rather	Not Very	Yes	No
I always go	N=	19	27	19	28	22	25	18	19	8	13	14	12	32	15	20	27
	%=	2.9	4.1	3.3	3.7	3.8	3.4	2.8	3.6	2.6	3.4	3.6	4.5	4.1	2.7	5.2	2.8
I frequently go	N=	78	72	34	113	61	86	66	65	20	42	50	37	106	41	52	97
	%=	11.5	11.0	6.0	15.3	10.6	11.8	10.2	12.4	6.5	11.1	13.2	14.2	13.9	7.5	13.7	10.3
I sometimes go	N=	212	227	174	265	179	253	219	171	70	130	134	104	281	155	134	305
	%=	31.4	34.8	30.3	35.8	31.1	34.5	34.1	32.4	23.2	34.0	35.4	39.7	36.6	28.2	35.0	32.3
I seldom go	N=	235	181	203	204	182	228	222	148	108	127	123	58	218	194	123	293
	%=	34.9	27.8	35.4	27.5	31.7	31.0	34.5	28.1	35.9	33.2	32.4	22.1	28.4	35.4	32.2	31.0
I never go	N=	130	145	143	130	132	142	118	124	96	70	58	51	130	144	53	222
	%=	19.3	22.2	24.9	17.6	22.9	19.3	18.4	23.6	31.7	18.3	15.3	19.5	17.0	26.2	14.0	23.5
No answer	N=	66	88	31	123	101	51	50	73	44	51	40	19	101	51	60	94
Analyzed Respondents	N=	674	652	572	740	576	733	642	526	301	382	380	263	767	549	382	944
	%=	100.0	99.9	99.9	99.9	100.1	100.0	100.0	100.1	99.9	100.0	99.9	100.0	100.0	100.0	100.1	99.9

TABLE 37

If someone dies WHO IS ONLY AN ACQUAINTANCE, would you attend the funeral service?

		SEX		AGE		EDUCATION			INCOME			REGION				RELIGIOUS			ARRG. FNRL.	
		M	F	Under 45	45 & Over	HS or Less	Some Clge/ More	8000 to 19999	20000 & Over	East	Mid-west	South	West	Rather	Not Very	Yes	No
I always go	N=	2	14	4	12	9	7	5	7	4	4	5	3	12	4	10	6
	%=	0.3	2.2	0.7	1.7	1.6	1.0	1.0	1.1	1.3	1.1	1.3	1.1	1.6	0.7	2.6	0.6
I frequently go	N=	25	26	12	39	30	22	18	24	5	15	15	17	34	17	23	29
	%=	3.8	4.0	2.1	5.4	5.2	3.0	3.4	3.7	1.6	4.0	3.9	6.3	4.6	3.1	6.0	3.1
I sometimes go	N=	99	113	64	146	95	112	90	91	24	61	77	50	153	57	75	137
	%=	14.9	17.6	11.3	20.1	16.7	15.6	17.2	14.5	8.0	16.5	20.4	19.0	20.2	10.5	19.7	14.8
I seldom go	N=	206	187	180	207	157	228	156	203	68	129	118	79	233	155	100	292
	%=	31.0	29.1	31.6	28.6	27.6	31.6	29.8	32.3	22.8	34.9	31.1	29.8	30.8	28.7	26.5	31.5
I never go	N=	332	303	309	320	279	353	254	304	196	161	163	115	323	309	171	464
	%=	50.0	47.1	54.3	44.2	49.0	48.8	48.7	48.4	66.1	43.5	43.2	43.6	42.8	57.0	45.2	50.0
No answer	N=	76	97	34	139	108	63	77	65	49	64	42	18	112	58	63	109
Analyzed	N=	664	643	569	725	569	722	522	628	296	369	378	264	756	542	379	928
Respondents	%=	100.0	100.0	100.0	100.0	100.1	100.0	100.1	100.0	99.8	100.0	99.9	99.8	100.0	100.0	100.0	100.0

TABLE 38

Do you have a preferred funeral home, one that you would probably turn to if needed?

		SEX		AGE		EDUCATION		INCOME		REGION				RELIGIOUS		ARRG. FNRL.	
		M	F	Under 45	45 & Over	HS or Less	Some Clge/ More	8000 to 19999	20000 & Over	East	Mid-west	South	West	Rather	Not Very	Yes	No
Yes	N=	421	485	276	623	452	444	370	411	211	289	274	133	575	326	341	565
	%=	57.1	66.1	46.0	72.5	67.3	56.7	62.0	59.6	61.2	66.8	65.6	48.0	66.7	54.5	77.8	54.7
No	N=	317	249	324	236	219	339	227	279	134	144	144	145	287	272	97	468
	%=	42.9	33.9	54.0	27.5	32.7	43.3	38.0	40.4	38.8	33.2	34.4	52.0	33.3	45.5	22.2	45.3
No answer	N=	2	6	3	5	6	2	3	3	1	1	2	4	6	2	4	4
Analyzed Respondents	N=	738	734	600	859	671	783	596	690	344	433	417	278	862	598	439	1033
	%=	100.0	100.0	100.0	100.0	100.0	100.0	100.0	100.0	100.0	100.0	100.0	100.0	100.0	100.0	100.0	100.0

TABLE 39

How would you rate that funeral home?

		SEX		AGE		EDUCATION		INCOME		REGION				RELIGIOUS			ARRG. FNRL.	
		M	F	Under 45	45 & Over	HS or Less	Some Clge/ More	8000 to 19999	20000 & Over	East	Mid-west	South	West	Rather	Not Very	Yes	No	
Excellent	N=	223	275	136	360	256	241	209	207	123	151	157	67	330	166	198	300	
	%=	53.2	57.2	49.5	58.3	57.3	54.5	57.1	50.7	58.7	52.3	57.8	51.6	57.6	51.7	58.4	53.5	
Good	N=	190	197	132	250	186	192	153	194	83	136	110	59	234	150	137	250	
	%=	45.4	41.0	47.9	40.4	41.6	43.3	41.8	47.4	39.4	47.0	40.4	45.4	40.8	46.5	40.4	44.6	
Fair	N=	6	9	7	8	5	10	4	8	4	2	5	4	9	6	4	11	
	%=	1.4	1.9	2.5	1.3	1.1	2.2	1.1	1.9	1.9	0.7	1.8	3.0	1.6	1.8	1.2	1.9	
No answer	N=	2	4	1	5	5	1	4	2	1	—	2	3	2	4	2	4	
Analyzed	N=	419	481	275	618	447	443	366	409	210	289	272	130	573	322	339	561	
Respondents	%=	100.0	100.1	99.9	100.0	100.0	100.0	100.0	100.0	100.0	100.0	100.0	100.0	100.0	100.0	100.0	100.0	

TABLE 40

Do you think that funeral homes in general should advertise?

		SEX		AGE		EDUCATION		INCOME		REGION				RELIGIOUS			ARRG. FNRL.	
		M	F	Under 45	45 & Over	HS or Less	Some Clge/ More	8000 to 19999	20000 & Over	East	Mid-west	South	West	Rather	Not Very	Yes	No
No	N=	142	141	131	150	150	130	114	121	73	84	74	52	171	111	81	202
	%=	19.4	19.2	21.9	17.6	22.5	16.6	19.2	17.6	21.2	19.6	17.9	18.6	19.8	18.8	18.6	19.6
Yes	N=	247	199	174	271	173	265	188	216	112	133	124	77	270	166	141	305
	%	33.8	27.0	29.1	31.8	25.9	33.9	31.6	31.4	32.6	31.0	30.0	27.3	31.3	28.1	32.2	29.6
Undecided/ no opinion	N=	342	396	293	433	344	386	293	351	159	212	215	152	422	315	215	523
	%=	46.8	53.8	49.0	50.7	51.5	49.5	49.2	51.0	46.2	49.4	52.1	54.1	48.9	53.2	49.2	50.8
No answer	N=	10	4	5	9	10	4	4	5	2	5	6	1	6	8	6	8
Analyzed Respondents	N=	730	736	598	855	667	781	596	688	343	429	413	281	862	592	437	1029
	%=	100.0	100.0	100.0	100.1	99.9	100.0	100.0	100.0	100.0	100.0	100.0	100.0	100.0	100.1	100.0	100.0

TABLE 41

What price of casket would you probably select for yourself?

		SEX		AGE		EDUCATION		INCOME		REGION				RELIGIOUS		ARRG. FNRL	
		M	F	Under 45	45 & Over	HS or Less	Some Clge/More	8000 to 19999	20000 & Over	East	Mid-west	South	West	Rather	Not Very	Yes	No
One that's above my income bracket	N=	4	4	3	3	4	4	5	2	--	4	3	1	3	5	4	4
	%=	0.5	0.6	0.5	0.4	0.6	0.5	0.9	0.3	--	0.9	0.7	0.4	0.4	0.9	0.9	0.4
One that's within my income bracket	N=	355	418	268	503	398	361	335	332	181	254	230	108	499	271	286	487
	%=	50.0	59.0	45.5	61.5	61.6	47.9	58.0	49.7	54.8	61.0	56.2	40.9	59.7	47.2	68.3	48.7
One that's below my income bracket	N=	153	103	114	137	94	163	85	139	52	72	84	48	153	101	45	211
	%=	21.6	14.5	19.3	16.7	14.5	21.6	14.8	20.7	15.8	17.2	20.6	18.3	18.3	17.6	10.8	21.1
Would not want a casket	N=	87	90	100	78	56	121	69	94	45	30	42	60	72	103	40	137
	%=	12.3	12.7	16.9	9.5	8.7	16.0	12.0	14.1	13.7	7.1	10.3	22.9	8.6	18.0	9.6	13.7
Undecided/ no opinion	N=	111	94	105	98	95	105	83	101	52	57	49	46	108	93	43	162
	%=	15.6	13.3	17.8	11.9	14.6	13.9	14.3	15.1	15.7	13.7	12.1	17.6	13.0	16.3	10.3	16.1
No answer	N=	29	31	13	45	30	30	22	25	15	17	10	19	33	27	24	37
Analyzed Respondents	N=	711	709	590	818	647	754	578	668	331	417	409	263	836	573	419	1001
	%=	100.0	100.1	100.0	100.0	100.0	99.9	100.0	99.9	100.0	99.9	99.9	100.1	100.0	100.0	99.9	100.0

TABLE 42

What price of casket would you probably select for your spouse?

		SEX		AGE		EDUCATION		INCOME			REGION					RELIGIOUS			ARRG. FNRL.	
		M	F	Under 45	45 & Over	HS or Less	Some Clge/ More	8000 to 19999	20000 & Over	East	Mid-west	South	West	Rather	Not Very	Yes	No
One that's above my income bracket	N=	16	12	16	12	14	14	12	12	4	16	5	3	16	12	6	15
	%=	2.2	2.0	2.8	1.6	2.3	2.0	2.2	1.8	1.3	4.1	1.3	1.2	2.1	2.2	1.9	1.6
One that's within my income bracket	N=	435	396	313	516	404	414	351	386	186	264	254	127	503	321	226	564
	%=	61.5	65.9	55.7	69.9	67.7	59.5	65.7	60.0	59.9	68.2	69.3	52.1	66.2	59.8	72.8	60.1
One that's below my income bracket	N=	80	64	63	77	55	88	56	78	36	41	39	27	97	46	27	114
	%=	11.3	10.6	11.2	10.4	9.3	12.7	10.5	12.1	11.7	10.7	10.8	10.9	12.8	8.6	8.6	12.2
Would not want a casket	N=	76	59	76	57	43	91	51	74	34	22	27	52	52	81	25	106
	%=	10.7	9.8	13.5	7.7	7.3	13.1	9.6	11.5	11.1	5.6	7.2	21.4	6.9	15.0	8.2	11.3
Undecided/ no opinion	N=	101	70	94	77	80	88	64	94	50	44	41	35	92	77	26	139
	%=	14.3	11.6	16.8	10.4	13.4	12.7	12.0	14.6	16.1	11.4	11.3	14.5	12.1	14.4	8.5	14.3
Not applicable or no answer	N=	33	139	41	125	81	90	62	50	35	47	53	38	109	63	73	100
Analyzed Respondents	N=	707	601	562	738	596	695	535	643	311	387	366	244	760	537	310	938

TABLE 43

What price of casket would you probably select for your parents or other family members?

		SEX		AGE		EDUCATION		INCOME		REGION				RELIGIOUS		ARRG. FNRL.	
		M	F	Under 45	45 & Over	HS or Less	Some Clge/More	8000 to 19999	20000 & Over	East	Mid-west	South	West	Rather	Not Very	Yes	No
One that's above my income bracket	N=	12	17	23	6	10	19	16	6	7	10	8	4	17	12	3	22
	%=	1.9	3.0	4.0	1.0	1.9	2.9	3.4	1.0	2.5	2.9	2.5	1.8	2.6	2.4	1.1	2.6
One that's within my income bracket	N=	394	378	348	423	357	403	314	371	176	254	217	125	441	326	214	529
	%=	65.3	67.5	61.5	71.7	69.5	63.4	67.5	63.8	64.0	72.9	67.5	57.2	67.0	65.3	76.5	63.0
One that's below my income bracket	N=	72	48	58	58	39	78	35	72	30	25	39	25	80	39	29	88
	%=	11.9	8.6	10.2	9.9	7.7	12.3	7.6	12.3	11.0	7.0	12.3	11.7	12.2	7.9	10.5	10.5
Would not want a casket	N=	21	25	27	18	16	31	21	24	11	6	11	19	20	27	3	41
	%=	3.5	4.5	4.7	3.0	3.1	4.8	4.5	4.0	3.9	1.7	3.4	8.6	3.0	5.3	1.1	4.9
Undecided/ no opinion	N=	105	92	110	85	92	105	79	110	51	54	46	45	100	95	30	159
	%=	17.4	16.4	19.5	14.4	17.8	16.5	17.0	18.9	18.6	15.5	14.4	20.7	15.2	19.1	10.9	18.9
Not applicable or no answer	N=	136	180	38	275	162	149	135	110	70	85	99	63	210	111	118	199
Analyzed Respondents	N=	604	560	565	589	514	636	465	582	275	349	321	219	658	499	280	839

TABLE 44

What kind of casket material would you probably select for yourself?

		SEX		AGE		EDUCATION		INCOME		REGION				RELIGIOUS		ARRG. FNRL.	
		M	F	Under 45	45 & Over	HS or Less	Some Clge/More	8000 to 19999	20000 & Over	East	Mid-west	South	West	Rather	Not Very	Yes	No
Wood	N=	179	145	111	205	130	190	129	146	98	109	53	63	192	130	83	241
	%=	25.3	20.7	18.9	25.4	20.2	25.4	22.5	22.1	29.5	26.7	13.2	24.0	23.2	22.7	20.0	24.3
Steel	N=	140	93	71	161	121	108	94	103	37	78	84	33	148	82	88	144
	%=	19.8	13.3	12.2	20.0	18.8	14.4	16.4	15.5	11.2	19.0	20.9	12.8	18.0	14.3	21.3	14.6
Stainless Steel	N=	43	39	44	37	36	43	32	44	18	20	39	5	57	25	30	52
	%=	6.0	5.6	7.5	4.6	5.5	5.8	5.7	6.7	5.3	4.8	9.7	1.9	6.9	4.3	7.1	5.3
Precious Metal	N=	41	60	41	54	69	28	49	40	25	39	30	7	64	36	50	50
	%=	5.8	8.6	6.9	6.7	10.8	3.7	8.6	6.1	7.4	9.6	7.3	2.6	7.8	6.4	12.2	5.1
Fiberglass	N=	56	35	39	52	36	56	38	46	18	24	28	22	57	33	22	70
	%=	8.0	5.0	6.7	6.5	5.5	7.5	6.7	6.9	5.3	6.0	6.8	8.2	6.9	5.8	5.2	7.0
No casket	N=	72	82	92	62	52	101	61	82	40	24	33	56	57	94	37	117
	%=	10.2	11.7	15.6	7.7	8.2	13.6	10.7	12.3	12.2	5.8	8.3	21.4	7.0	16.5	8.8	11.8
Don't know	N=	177	247	189	234	199	221	169	202	97	115	136	76	250	171	106	318
	%=	25.0	35.2	32.2	29.1	30.9	29.6	29.5	30.4	29.0	28.1	33.7	29.0	30.2	30.0	25.4	32.0
No answer	N=	33	39	15	57	34	38	26	29	13	25	15	20	42	29	28	44
Analyzed Respondents	N=	707	701	588	807	643	746	574	664	333	409	404	262	826	571	415	993
	%=	100.1	100.1	100.0	100.0	99.9	100.0	100.1	100.0	99.9	100.0	99.9	99.9	100.0	100.0	100.0	100.1

TABLE 45

What kind of casket material would you probably select for your spouse?

		SEX		AGE		EDUCATION		INCOME		REGION					RELIGIOUS			ARRG. FNRL.	
		M	F	Under 45	45 & Over	HS or Less	Some Clge/ More	8000 to 19999	20000 & Over	East	Mid-west	South	West	Rather	Not Very	Yes	No
Wood	N=	155	117	94	172	112	156	109	126	84	92	42	53	154	117	66	198
	%=	22.3	20.1	17.1	24.1	19.2	23.1	20.8	20.0	27.3	24.7	11.9	22.1	20.6	22.3	21.8	21.5
Steel	N=	142	80	68	154	112	106	96	104	33	75	79	34	137	81	63	144
	%=	20.4	13.7	12.2	21.6	19.2	15.6	18.3	16.5	10.8	19.9	22.3	14.3	18.5	15.6	20.7	15.7
Stainless Steel	N=	50	34	46	38	38	43	32	46	21	22	38	4	60	24	25	59
	%=	7.3	5.8	8.3	5.4	6.6	6.4	6.2	7.3	6.7	5.8	10.8	1.7	8.1	4.7	8.1	6.4
Precious Metal	N=	58	68	64	60	77	47	56	59	32	49	32	14	74	52	43	71
	%=	8.4	11.7	11.6	8.4	13.2	7.0	10.7	9.4	10.3	13.2	8.9	5.7	10.0	10.0	14.1	7.7
Fiberglass	N=	49	23	29	42	28	44	30	37	12	16	24	21	47	24	14	57
	%=	7.0	3.9	5.3	5.9	4.7	6.5	5.8	5.9	3.8	4.2	6.7	8.6	6.3	4.7	4.6	6.2
No casket	N=	62	54	69	45	40	77	44	65	28	23	17	48	44	70	27	89
	%=	8.9	9.3	12.4	6.3	6.8	11.3	8.4	10.3	9.2	6.1	4.7	20.1	6.0	13.3	9.1	9.6
Don't know	N=	179	207	183	203	178	204	157	192	98	98	123	66	227	154	65	303
	%=	25.7	35.5	33.1	28.3	30.4	30.1	29.9	30.5	31.9	26.2	34.7	27.5	30.6	29.5	21.6	32.9
Not applicable or no answer	N=	44	157	49	149	92	108	74	64	37	60	64	42	124	77	84	118

TABLE 46

What type of casket material would you probably select for your parents or other family members?

		SEX		AGE		EDUCATION		INCOME		REGION				RELIGIOUS		ARRG. FNRL.	
		M	F	Under 45	45 & Over	HS or Less	Some Clge/ More	8000 to 19999	20000 & Over	East	Mid-west	South	West	Rather	Not Very	Yes	No
Wood	N=	142	96	106	128	89	145	97	106	75	77	36	50	121	117	55	177
	%=	23.4	17.8	18.7	22.6	17.4	23.3	21.2	18.2	27.4	22.4	11.4	23.3	18.6	24.0	20.5	21.2
Steel	N=	124	87	81	131	110	97	87	104	28	78	69	36	130	79	62	139
	%=	20.5	16.1	14.2	23.1	21.7	15.6	19.1	17.9	10.3	22.7	21.9	17.0	20.0	16.1	23.1	16.6
Stainless Steel	N=	47	37	52	31	34	47	31	46	18	22	37	7	54	30	24	58
	%=	7.7	6.9	9.2	5.6	6.8	7.6	6.9	7.9	6.4	6.3	11.9	3.2	8.3	6.1	8.8	7.0
Precious Metal	N=	47	72	65	49	74	42	53	54	37	44	24	14	74	44	43	68
	%=	7.7	13.4	11.5	8.7	14.6	6.8	11.7	9.3	13.3	13.0	7.6	6.4	11.4	9.1	15.9	8.2
Fiberglass	N=	43	18	28	32	21	40	23	34	14	12	20	16	39	22	9	52
	%=	7.1	3.3	5.0	5.7	4.1	6.4	4.9	5.9	5.0	3.4	6.3	7.3	6.0	4.4	3.3	6.2
No casket	N=	17	24	24	16	10	31	14	27	9	7	6	20	20	22	6	35
	%=	2.9	4.5	4.2	2.8	2.0	5.1	3.1	4.7	3.2	2.0	1.9	9.2	3.0	4.5	2.2	4.2
Don't know	N=	186	205	212	178	170	220	152	210	94	103	122	72	212	175	70	305
	%=	30.8	38.0	37.3	31.4	33.4	35.2	33.2	36.0	34.3	30.1	39.0	33.5	32.6	35.9	26.1	36.6
Not applicable or no answer	N=	134	201	35	299	169	162	142	110	70	92	105	67	218	112	131	205
Analyzed Respondents	N=	606	539	568	565	508	623	458	582	275	342	313	214	649	488	268	833
	%=																

TABLE 47

How much difference would what the casket is made of make to you?

		SEX		AGE		EDUCATION		INCOME		REGION				RELIGIOUS		ARRG. FNRL.	
		M	F	Under 45	45 & Over	HS or Less	Some Clge/More	8000 to 19999	20000 & Over	East	Mid-west	South	West	Rather	Not Very	Yes	No
Would make a lot of difference	N=	62	59	48	71	75	43	50	48	33	34	45	9	80	41	45	76
	%=	8.8	8.3	8.3	8.7	11.4	5.8	8.7	7.3	9.7	8.3	11.3	3.3	9.6	7.3	10.9	7.6
Would make some difference	N=	105	138	97	146	126	117	95	111	65	76	67	35	153	88	91	152
	%=	14.8	19.4	16.5	17.9	19.2	15.8	16.4	16.8	19.4	18.3	16.8	12.9	18.3	15.4	21.7	15.2
Would make only a small difference	N=	130	171	121	174	141	152	121	144	65	96	85	55	183	114	76	225
	%=	18.4	24.1	20.7	21.3	21.6	20.4	21.0	21.7	19.4	23.2	21.3	20.5	21.8	20.1	18.2	22.5
Would make no difference to me	N=	410	342	319	427	312	432	312	359	173	207	202	170	421	325	206	546
	%=	58.0	48.2	54.5	52.2	47.7	58.0	54.0	54.2	51.5	50.1	50.6	63.3	50.3	57.2	49.2	54.7
No answer	N=	33	30	18	45	23	40	21	30	10	21	20	13	32	31	25	38
Analyzed Respondents	N=	707	710	585	818	654	744	579	663	336	413	400	269	837	569	418	999
	%=	100.0	100.0	100.0	100.1	99.9	100.0	100.1	100.0	100.0	99.9	100.0	100.0	100.0	100.0	100.0	100.0

TABLE 48

If it were possible to save 20% or so by buying a casket from some place other than a funeral home, would you?

| | | SEX | | AGE | | EDUCATION | | INCOME | | REGION | | | | RELIGIOUS | | | ARRG. FNRL | |
		M	F	Under 45	45 & Over	HS or Less	Some Clge/ More	8000 to 19999	20000 & Over	East	Mid-west	South	West	Rather	Not Very	Yes	No
Definitely	N=	183	148	167	161	149	180	144	154	79	86	91	75	187	143	81	250
	%=	25.5	20.9	28.3	19.7	22.8	23.9	24.9	23.0	23.1	20.8	22.2	28.9	22.3	25.0	19.2	24.9
Probably	N=	198	181	163	213	151	223	135	196	81	109	115	74	229	148	99	280
	%=	27.6	25.6	27.5	26.0	23.1	29.6	23.4	29.2	23.8	26.2	28.2	28.4	27.2	25.8	23.6	27.9
Undecided/ no opinion	N=	173	232	180	219	194	206	154	197	109	106	122	68	224	176	120	284
	%=	24.1	32.8	30.5	26.7	29.7	27.4	26.7	29.4	32.2	25.3	29.8	26.3	26.7	30.8	28.5	28.4
Probably not	N=	122	112	64	168	109	120	113	93	54	87	63	31	150	81	85	150
	%=	17.1	15.8	10.9	20.5	16.7	15.9	19.6	13.9	15.9	20.8	15.4	11.8	17.8	14.1	20.1	14.9
Definitely not	N=	41	34	17	58	50	25	31	31	17	29	18	12	50	24	36	38
	%=	5.7	4.8	2.8	7.1	7.7	3.3	5.4	4.6	4.9	6.8	4.3	4.6	6.0	4.3	8.6	3.8
No answer	N=	23	33	12	44	25	32	22	22	6	17	11	23	29	28	21	36
Analyzed Respondents	N=	717	707	591	819	652	753	578	671	339	417	408	259	839	572	422	1002
	%=	100.0	99.9	100.0	100.0	100.0	100.1	100.0	100.1	99.9	99.9	99.9	100.0	100.0	100.0	100.0	99.9

TABLE 49

What is your opinion about using a rental casket for display of the body and then using an inexpensive, plain container for placing the body in its final resting place?

		SEX		AGE		EDUCATION			INCOME			REGION					RELIGIOUS			ARRG. FNRL	
		M	F	Under 45	45 & Over	HS or Less	Some Clge/ More	8000 to 19999	20000 & Over	East	Mid-west	South	West	Rather	Not Very	Yes	No
Sounds awful and I'm totally against it	N=	184	257	148	294	271	166	204	158	102	123	154	62	279	163	158	283
	%=	25.7	35.9	24.9	35.5	41.3	21.8	35.1	23.5	30.1	29.7	37.4	23.3	32.9	28.3	37.2	28.1
Sounds okay for some people but not for me	N=	144	143	133	148	132	147	120	126	76	77	81	53	183	100	79	208
	%=	20.0	20.0	22.4	17.9	20.2	19.3	20.7	18.7	22.4	18.5	19.6	20.0	21.7	17.4	18.6	20.6
Sounds interesting and I might consider it	N=	169	132	148	150	97	202	92	186	72	102	70	57	161	136	86	215
	%=	23.5	18.5	24.9	18.1	14.8	26.6	15.8	27.6	21.2	24.6	17.0	21.4	19.0	23.7	20.2	21.3
Sounds good and I would want to use a rental casket	N=	85	36	50	69	41	80	48	69	27	28	32	33	58	64	29	92
	%=	11.9	5.0	8.4	8.4	6.3	10.6	8.3	10.3	8.1	6.8	7.8	12.5	6.8	11.1	6.9	9.1
Undecided/ no opinion	N=	136	147	115	166	115	164	117	134	62	85	75	61	166	112	73	210
	%=	18.9	20.6	19.4	20.1	17.5	21.7	20.2	19.9	18.3	20.4	18.2	22.9	19.6	19.5	17.1	20.8
No answer	N=	21	25	9	37	21	26	18	20	7	18	7	15	22	25	18	29
Analyzed	N=	719	715	594	826	656	759	582	673	339	416	412	267	846	575	425	1009

TABLE 50

If it were up to you, what would you probably arrange for yourself?

		SEX		AGE		EDUCATION		INCOME		REGION				RELIGIOUS		ARRG. FNRL	
		M	F	Under 45	45 & Over	HS or Less	Some Clge/More	8000 to 19999	20000 & Over	East	Mid-west	South	West	Rather	Not Very	Yes	No
Burial in ground	N=	410	435	330	505	462	370	364	353	200	269	264	112	557	283	271	573
	%=	56.9	60.4	55.6	60.6	70.0	48.6	62.1	52.5	59.1	64.5	64.1	41.0	66.1	48.3	63.5	56.6
Cremation	N=	163	128	129	159	91	200	103	162	71	60	65	96	112	175	80	211
	%=	22.6	17.8	21.7	19.0	13.8	26.3	17.5	24.1	20.9	14.4	15.7	34.9	13.3	29.9	18.7	20.9
Donation to science	N=	62	79	60	81	39	101	57	77	28	41	48	25	84	57	38	103
	%=	8.6	11.0	10.2	9.7	5.9	13.2	9.8	11.4	8.2	9.8	11.7	9.0	10.0	9.8	8.8	10.2
Entombment above ground	N=	33	28	17	44	27	32	27	25	17	14	20	11	34	25	19	42
	%=	4.6	3.9	2.8	5.3	4.0	4.3	4.6	3.6	4.9	3.3	4.8	4.0	4.1	4.2	4.4	4.2
Burial at sea	N=	8	1	7	2	1	8	2	7	—	4	1	4	1	8	2	7
	%=	1.1	0.1	1.1	0.2	0.2	1.0	0.3	1.0	—	0.9	0.2	1.4	0.1	1.3	0.5	0.7
Other	N=	6	1	4	3	2	5	2	5	2	2	1	2	5	2	—	7
	%=	0.8	0.1	0.7	0.4	0.3	0.6	0.3	0.7	0.6	0.5	0.2	0.7	0.6	0.3	—	0.7
Undecided/ no opinion	N=	39	48	47	40	39	46	32	44	22	28	13	25	50	36	18	69
	%=	5.4	6.7	8.0	4.7	5.8	6.1	5.4	6.6	6.4	6.6	3.2	9.0	5.9	6.2	4.2	6.8
No answer	N=	19	20	9	30	17	23	14	20	7	17	8	8	25	14	16	24
Analyzed Respondents	N=	720	720	594	833	660	762	586	673	339	417	411	274	843	586	427	1013
	%=	100.0	100.0	100.1	99.9	100.0	100.1	100.0	99.9	100.1	100.0	99.9	100.0	100.1	100.0	100.1	100.1

TABLE 51

If it were up to you, what would you probably arrange for your spouse?

		SEX		AGE		EDUCATION		INCOME		REGION				RELIGIOUS		ARRG. FNRL	
		M	F	Under 45	45 & Over	HS or Less	Some Clge/More	8000 to 19999	20000 & Over	East	Mid-west	South	West	Rather	Not Very	Yes	No
Burial in ground	N=	458	430	358	524	453	419	381	400	206	293	277	112	572	313	275	613
	%=	63.4	66.6	62.2	67.3	73.0	57.4	68.3	60.2	63.6	73.5	71.9	43.1	71.3	56.2	70.2	62.8
Cremation	N=	142	102	110	128	75	169	83	141	57	45	49	92	100	140	71	173
	%=	19.6	15.8	19.1	16.4	12.1	23.1	14.8	21.3	17.6	11.4	12.8	35.4	12.5	25.1	18.0	17.7
Donation to science	N=	41	25	28	38	22	44	29	35	17	15	19	16	37	28	12	54
	%=	5.6	3.9	4.8	4.9	3.5	6.1	5.1	5.3	5.2	3.7	4.8	6.0	4.7	5.1	3.0	5.5
Entombment above ground	N=	45	21	23	43	27	37	28	31	21	18	16	11	34	29	16	50
	%=	6.2	3.3	3.9	5.5	4.3	5.1	4.9	4.7	6.6	4.4	4.1	4.1	4.3	5.3	4.0	5.1
Burial at sea	N=	2	5	2	5	2	5	1	4	--	--	2	5	5	2	--	7
	%=	0.3	0.8	0.3	0.6	0.3	0.7	0.2	0.6	--	--	0.5	1.9	0.6	0.3	--	0.7
Other	N=	--	3	1	2	2	1	1	1	2	--	1	--	2	1	--	3
	%=	--	0.5	0.2	0.3	0.3	0.1	0.2	0.2	0.6	--	0.3	--	0.2	0.2	--	0.3
Undecided/ no opinion	N=	35	60	54	39	40	54	36	51	21	28	22	25	51	43	19	76
	%=	4.8	9.3	9.5	5.0	6.5	7.5	6.4	7.7	6.4	7.0	5.6	9.5	6.3	7.8	4.8	7.8
No answer	N=	17	94	27	84	56	56	42	29	22	35	34	21	67	44	51	61
Analyzed Respondents	N=	722	646	576	779	621	729	558	664	324	399	385	261	801	556	392	976
	%=	99.9	100.2	100.0	100.0	100.0	100.0	99.9	100.0	100.0	100.0	100.0	100.0	99.9	100.0	100.0	99.9

TABLE 52

If it were up to you, what would you probably arrange for someone in your immediate family or a close friend?

		SEX		AGE		EDUCATION		INCOME		REGION					RELIGIOUS			ARRG. FNRL	
		M	F	Under 45	45 & Over	HS or Less	Some Clge/ More	8000 to 19999	20000 & Over	East	Mid-west	South	West	Rather	Not Very	Yes	No
Burial in ground	N=	454	428	420	459	417	449	379	412	204	285	275	118	545	332	255	627
	%=	68.8	70.0	71.1	68.7	74.3	64.7	74.1	64.8	67.9	76.7	76.7	49.2	75.7	61.2	72.0	68.4
Cremation	N=	82	61	72	63	43	100	44	88	38	20	28	56	47	92	43	99
	%=	12.4	10.0	12.2	9.4	7.6	14.4	8.7	13.9	12.8	5.3	7.9	23.3	6.6	17.1	12.2	10.8
Donation to science	N=	25	14	15	24	14	25	18	21	10	9	14	7	27	12	9	30
	%=	3.8	2.3	2.5	3.7	2.5	3.7	3.5	3.2	3.3	2.4	3.8	2.9	3.8	2.2	2.5	3.3
Entombment above ground	N=	27	19	21	25	21	25	16	27	14	12	11	10	20	26	16	31
	%=	4.1	3.1	3.5	3.8	3.7	3.7	3.1	4.3	4.6	3.2	3.0	4.1	2.7	4.9	4.4	3.3
Burial at sea	N=	2	—	—	2	—	2	—	2	—	—	—	2	—	2	—	2
	%=	0.3	—	—	0.3	—	0.3	—	0.3	—	—	—	0.8	—	0.4	—	0.2
Other	N=	2	—	—	2	—	2	—	2	2	—	—	—	—	2	2	—
	%=	0.3	—	—	0.3	—	0.3	—	0.3	0.6	—	—	—	—	0.4	0.5	—
Undecided/ no opinion	N=	68	89	63	92	67	90	54	84	32	47	31	47	80	76	30	127
	%=	10.3	14.6	10.7	13.8	12.0	13.0	10.6	13.2	10.8	12.5	8.5	19.7	11.2	14.0	8.4	13.9
No answer	N=	80	129	13	196	116	91	88	57	46	61	60	41	148	58	88	121
Analyzed Respondents	N=	660	611	590	668	561	694	511	636	300	372	359	240	720	542	355	917
	%=	100.0	100.0	100.0	100.0	100.1	100.1	100.0	100.0	100.0	100.1	99.9	100.0	100.0	100.2	100.0	99.9

TABLE 53

There are several ways to inform people arranging funerals about the price. Which of the following pricing methods would you prefer, assuming that the total price would be the same with any of the methods?

		SEX		AGE		EDUCATION			INCOME			REGION					RELIGIOUS			ARRG. FNRL.	
		M	F	Under 45	45 & Over	HS or Less	Some Clge/ More	8000 to 19999	20000 & Over	East	Mid-west	South	West	Rather	Not Very	Yes	No
Unit Pricing	N=	229	259	158	330	257	223	215	187	108	144	143	93	298	189	147	341
	%=	31.9	36.1	26.8	39.6	39.4	29.2	36.7	27.7	32.0	34.3	35.4	33.9	35.4	32.5	34.4	33.8
Functional Pricing	N=	122	114	102	128	101	134	89	123	60	70	63	43	133	101	70	167
	%=	17.0	15.9	17.4	15.4	15.4	17.5	15.2	18.2	17.8	16.7	15.5	15.8	15.8	17.4	16.3	16.5
Itemized Pricing	N=	367	345	329	375	294	409	282	366	169	206	199	138	411	292	211	501
	%=	51.1	48.1	55.8	45.0	45.1	53.4	48.1	54.1	50.2	49.0	49.1	50.3	48.8	50.1	49.3	49.7
No answer	N=	21	22	14	30	25	19	14	17	8	14	14	8	26	18	15	29
Analyzed Respondents	N=	719	718	589	834	652	766	586	676	338	420	405	274	842	582	428	1009
	%=	100.0	100.1	100.0	100.0	99.9	100.1	100.0	100.0	100.0	100.0	100.0	100.0	100.0	100.0	100.0	100.0

TABLE 54

Suppose an extended payment plan were available from a funeral home that allowed the funeral to be paid for over a 1 to 3 year period AFTER the funeral. Assume the plan is confidentially and professionally handled, and charges the going interest rate for the extended payments. If you were making funeral arrangements, what would be your response to this plan?

	SEX		AGE		EDUCATION			INCOME		REGION					RELIGIOUS			ARRG. FNRL.	
	M	F	Under 45	45 & Over	HS or Less	Some Clge/ More	8000 to 19999	20000 & Over	East	Mid-west	South	West	Rather	Not Very	Yes	No
Would be almost certain to use extended N=	35	38	46	27	44	29	36	27	14	12	28	20		41	31	23	50
payment plan %=	4.8	5.2	7.8	3.1	6.6	3.7	6.1	3.9	4.1	2.8	6.6	7.1		4.7	5.3	5.2	4.9
Would probably use extended N=	115	90	95	110	99	101	95	77	54	52	55	43		119	82	47	157
payment plan %=	15.6	12.4	15.8	12.9	14.9	13.1	16.1	11.2	15.8	12.2	13.3	15.6		13.9	14.0	10.8	15.4
Indifferent/ don't know N=	221	214	225	207	189	242	171	207	102	134	125	74		242	194	112	323
%=	30.2	29.4	37.6	24.3	28.3	31.2	28.8	30.3	30.0	31.4	30.1	26.7		28.2	32.8	25.6	31.6
Would probably not use extended payment plan N=	171	201	140	228	172	196	138	190	79	115	110	69		232	136	115	257
%=	23.3	27.6	23.4	26.9	25.8	25.3	23.3	27.8	23.1	26.9	26.4	24.9		27.0	23.1	26.1	25.2
Would be almost certain not to use extended N=	188	185	92	276	160	207	153	183	92	114	96	71		225	145	142	232
payment plan %=	25.7	25.4	15.4	32.5	24.0	26.8	25.7	26.8	26.9	26.7	23.2	25.7		26.2	24.5	32.3	22.7
No answer N=	8	12	6	14	10	10	6	9	5	7	3	5		10	10	4	16
Analyzed Repondents N=	732	728	597	850	667	775	594	684	340	427	416	277		858	590	439	1021